MW00380654

Millio
Missi

Millionaire Mission

A 9-Step System to Level Up Your Finances and Build Wealth

BRIAN PRESTON
CPA, CFP®, PFS

Matt Holt Books
An Imprint of BenBella Books, Inc.
Dallas, TX

Matt Holt is an imprint of BenBella Books, Inc.
10440 N. Central Expressway
Suite 800
Dallas, TX 75231
benbellabooks.com
Send feedback to feedback@benbellabooks.com

Printed in the United States of America
10 9 8 7 6 5 4 3 2 1

Library of Congress Control Number: 2023048259
ISBN 9781637745014 (hardcover)
ISBN 9781637745021 (electronic)

Editing by Katie Dickman
Copyediting by Scott Calamar
Proofreading by Jenny Bridges and Lisa Story
Indexing by WordCo Indexing Services, Inc.
Text design and composition by PerfecType, Nashville, TN
Cover design by Micah Harris Jones of Love and Science
Cover image © Adobe Stock / dimj (rocket)
Printed by Lake Book Manufacturing

For Mom and Dad, for modeling an awesome marriage and life.
Dad, I wish you could read what you have created.
For Jennifer, Avery, and Emery—we don't have it all
figured out, but I love our quirky, abundant life.

Contents

PART 2

Beyond the Basics

Introduction

You Can Be Rich!—The Morrow Moment

I was in high school when my economics teacher uttered a sentence that changed my life forever.

I don't think Mr. Morrow chose to be our economics teacher. He was a veteran of the Vietnam War who retired from the military to teach and help coach our wrestling team. Rumors swirled among my classmates that he was once part of the Green Berets.

Mr. Morrow's class seemed like an unlikely source for life-changing financial advice; personal finance was not part of the curriculum. But one day he made one of those sidebar comments filled with wisdom that teachers tend to share. His guidance was simple but captured many of the fundamental elements of wealth building, and so it exploded like a stick of dynamite.

He told us, "I am so jealous of you. Every one of you can be a *millionaire* by the time you retire if you start investing one hundred dollars a month."

BOOM! With that one statement, Mr. Morrow yanked the elusive goal of becoming rich out of the "impossible" category and set it right in front of me—with little cost or complexity. He understood that *anyone can become rich!*

At the time, I was working in the drive-thru at the local Hardee's. Even though I was financially challenged (read: poor), I remember thinking that even I could save $100 a month. It wasn't until later that I realized Mr. Morrow was introducing us to the all-powerful force of compounding growth and the simple truth that small decisions today can have huge impacts in the future. He was also enforcing that the essential habits of being consistent and disciplined are rewarded many times over. Ever since, I have called this fundamental element of wealth building "The Morrow Moment."

That one statement, and that class in general, set me on a path to understand, learn, master, and wield the power of money to build wealth, happiness, and fulfillment. Unfortunately, as I started my journey, I quickly realized how muddy the waters of financial guidance and financial products were. I found there was a hodgepodge of competing financial approaches. Something one "guru" recommended was strictly forbidden by another.

I ultimately learned that there is a much simpler path to building significant wealth and living a life of abundance than we've been led to believe. We live in the greatest time to build wealth and fulfillment in the history of the world, but that is not shared publicly. We live in a world where many voices on the news, politicians, and social media are telling you that the system is stacked against you. I completely disagree with this fatalistic perspective. It goes back to my core belief that villains and victims do not win. However, victims can become the heroes of their own stories once they embrace that negatives and hardships may have contrarian opportunities.

The world needs an optimistic resource that shouts from the rooftop the knowledge, how-to steps, and big-picture mindset that are required to build wealth. I have poured my heart into creating this system so that it connects with anyone—regardless of income, age, and retirement target dates. How your journey started doesn't define how it ends.

This is where I step in to be your guide on this journey to building abundance. My journey from humble beginnings to wealth beyond what I could have ever imagined when I was sitting in Mr. Morrow's class can be yours, too. This is a system to help you accomplish your biggest goals and shape that inner voice. Not only have I used this system to create my personal success, I have used it to create wealth for clients of my billion-dollar financial planning firm for decades. We will make the good habits easy and the bad habits hard by focusing on the mindset of success and knowing exactly what the next step is in your plan.

This system pays special attention to mindset and motivation. Have you ever wondered why so many lottery winners go broke shortly after what appears to be a dream come true? Unfortunately, windfall wealth is full of buying and consuming goals (luxury goods, homes, and other extravagances) but short on the understanding that consumption can have empty endpoints and a helpless feeling of being without purpose.

This system will help you develop the behaviors, habits, and skills to avoid being one of those cautionary tales. You will not only accomplish your biggest goals, but this will become an epic journey that creates wisdom and contentment. By going on this journey, you will understand your "why" and purpose. When I speak of mindset, I am leaning toward helping you shape that inner voice and gatekeeper that, unfortunately, for most is more pessimistic than optimistic. My goal is to get you to refocus your inner voice to become your biggest cheerleader. This will shape your daily dialogue and you'll begin to ask, "What small decision today will maximize this moment and move me closer to my more beautiful tomorrow?" That simple shift in focus will wake up the beast within that will launch you toward your Millionaire Mission.

Here are a few of the key concepts you will hear more about in the pages of this book:

- Financial Order of Operations (FOO)—This nine-step system will teach you exactly what to do with your next dollar. This clarity and focus on maximization of the behaviors and habits will accelerate your path to wealth and financial freedom.
- 88x Over Principle—What is the potential of every dollar that comes into your possession? For a twentysomething, that one dollar has the potential to become $88 at retirement. For the twentysomething whose employer matches a percentage of their 401(k) contributions, that one dollar has the potential to become $176. Build this mindset, and you start thinking differently about how you spend your money. Spending $200/month instead of investing that money in your employer-sponsored plan with a match could cost your future self $4 million of additional resources at retirement (not a misprint).
- Army of Dollars—Now that you know the potential that one dollar holds, we can talk about recruiting more dollars into your army. Recruit and grow your Army of Dollars to the point that they work harder than you can. There is nothing better than wealth that works while you sleep and allows you to own your time. Leveraging your Army of Dollars allows you to do what you want, when you want, and live each day your way.
- Financial Mutant Mindset—I want to teach you to see a better way and develop a new financial identity because you see opportunities when others are fearful. Financial Mutants are contrarians that maximize the moments others miss because they are trapped in a herd mentality. This superpower will hone your critical-thinking skills and life habits to accelerate your wealth-building journey. It will also be the mindset that nudges that inner voice to ask: "What small decision today will maximize this moment and move me closer to my more beautiful tomorrow?!"

- Always Be Buying (ABB)—The world can be a scary and uncertain place, but there is a powerful approach that can help you stay on track, even in the middle of chaos. It's called "Always Be Buying" (ABB), and it holds the key to making your positive financial habits stick, regardless of what is going on around you. By implementing an automatic investment plan, you can navigate uncertainty with ease and set yourself up for success.
- Forced Scarcity—In a world driven by instant gratification and the allure of YOLO (You Only Live Once), it can be challenging to prioritize long-term financial success over short-term pleasures. However, there is a powerful tool that can help you overcome this struggle and propel you toward a brighter future. It's called "Forced Scarcity," and it holds the key to reshaping your cash flow, instilling discipline, and empowering you to make wiser financial choices. Save a little bit of today for a more beautiful tomorrow.
- Five Levels of Wealth—There is more to wealth than money. Wealth goes beyond a dollar amount (although that number is part of it) and extends to your mindset, contentment, and knowing your "why." I will walk you through the Five Levels of Wealth so you will know exactly where you are in the journey. Notice I referenced a journey and not a goal or endpoint. Goals are mile markers and not the final destination. Endpoints can be sad moments if you have accomplished a goal that was decades in the making and attention was not paid to the "why," purpose, and transition to the next chapter of the adventure. Understanding this subtle mindset difference will help you find a balance between reaching goals (mile markers) and developing a healthy relationship with the tool of money to know what it can and cannot do for you in the desire to reach happiness and fulfillment.

- More Beautiful Tomorrow—Imagine investing a small part of today to live a future life beyond your wildest dreams. This foundation of discipline and deferred gratification will keep you grounded and motivated. A very small deferment of your current comfort can have long-term exponential benefits, but it goes entirely against our consumer society. Having a vision toward building a more beautiful tomorrow can help keep the focus on becoming a builder over a consumer.
- Abundance Cycle—I feel that generosity is rewarded. Throughout my life, the more I have given away, the more I have received and been entrusted with. This core belief has led me to share this book so you can learn, apply, and grow your own personal wealth and success. Did I mention that by day I am a fee-only wealth manager? My businesses have exploded by sharing knowledge with no catch or ask until people reach a level of success that they need the services of my firm. This purity of message and passion is the motor that keeps this movement going.

Back to Mr. Morrow . . . and Beyond

Compounding growth is the driving force behind your Army of Dollars. It is, indeed, the eighth wonder of the world! It allows a little to go a long way and your money to work harder than you can. Mr. Morrow knew the three ingredients of wealth creation: discipline, money, and, most importantly, time. This book will help you develop fluency in all three, just as soon as you learn how to command and maximize every dollar in your army.

As I learned how to harness the power of compounding growth, I also learned that Mr. Morrow was slightly wrong, but in a good way. It's not just people under twenty who can reach millionaire status if they save consistently. Those who failed to immediately start investing in their twenties or thirties have not missed the opportunity to build wealth. The power of compounding growth is so powerful that it's never too late for someone to benefit from this amazing opportunity.

Ever since this "Morrow Moment," I wanted to be a teacher. I wanted to follow in the footsteps of my mother and grandmother and impact young lives just as they and Mr. Morrow had mine and those of so many other students. I was so passionate about this, I taught as a substitute through my college years. There is truly no greater experience than watching someone's eyes light up when they learn something new. It is exciting to share knowledge, hold the ladder of opportunity, and watch as the information alters a person's life path.

My dream of being a "traditional" teacher never came to fruition, but in 2005, I purchased my first Apple iPod and discovered a new medium called "podcasting." This tool allowed me to become a teacher in an unconventional way, and I loved that I didn't have to be confined to one classroom. I could reach people around the world just by sitting in front of a microphone.

Today, I find myself in front of a camera, co-hosting the popular YouTube channel I founded called *The Money Guy Show*. If you had told me the passion project I started in 2006 would lead to multiple cameras and microphones, hype buttons, and millions of hours of my financial content consumed each year, I would have laughed you out of the room. There is an insatiable hunger for what we share on *The Money Guy Show* because our viewers can sense something different: We always break down the numbers, we "eat our own cooking," and we feel that generosity is rewarded through something we call "the Abundance Cycle." I give away tons of free information to help my audience learn smart financial strategies, apply them, and grow to a level of success so that they can live their more beautiful tomorrows. The Abundance Cycle is that simple! Since there are no strings attached until success is reached, I have turned many skeptics into clients.

By day, I am the managing partner, a co-founder, and a fee-only financial advisor at a financial planning firm just south of Nashville, Tennessee, with a billion dollars' worth of assets under management. I have filled this book with knowledge learned from over 28 years of helping others make good financial decisions. I also have a background in public accounting; Certified Public Accountant (CPA)/Personal Financial Specialist (PFS), and CERTIFIED FINANCIAL PLANNER™ (CFP®) designations; and sixteen years of experience preparing and reviewing tax returns.

As you read this book, you will notice that I bring a unique perspective—one that represents decades of being around money and wealth creators—while still being approachable, because I know how it feels to be without money. My experience and education have shown me that most of what you think you know about money is wrong. The typical person has been misled concerning the relationship between money and happiness, as well as how to use money as an effective tool to build wealth and fulfillment. My goal is to help you fix those limiting beliefs and plant the seeds of knowledge that will help build your success.

Anyone Can Be Rich

There is a huge hidden benefit to having worked for three decades as a financial planner to wealthy families and businesses. I have had a front-row seat to how wealthy folks build their wealth. It is fascinating to learn how people make and spend their money. If you do this long enough, you start noticing highly successful people's habits and behaviors that anyone can apply, regardless of their current economic situation. I've also noticed there is an orderly flow to how you should work through financial decisions. I have used this knowledge to build my own wealth, so I know firsthand these steps are powerful. This book will not only share some of my own journey, but it will also teach you the nine tried-and-true steps that anyone wanting to build wealth, no matter their current net worth, can leverage.

When dealing with an "expert" who proposes a system to achieve success, I always ask, "Which came first, the chicken or the egg?" To clarify, I'm asking if the expert achieved success by selling a system or if they achieved success *because* of their system. I am a natural skeptic, so I must assure my readers this system was born from my journey and shared only after my successes. This knowledge has been so good for my clients and me. I have a burning passion to teach it to others so that more people can climb the ladder of financial success.

This book will not be light on actionable advice and concepts. Unfortunately, most financial content and self-proclaimed gurus are basic. For example, it is common sense that in order to start creating success, you will need to get out of debt. Balancing paying off your debt while taking advantage of your employer's free retirement money and funding a Roth Individual Retirement Arrangement (IRA) is on another level. There is a reason most of our clients are money masters, achievers, and analytical thinkers. We like to say, "The Money Guy family goes beyond common sense," and we always break down concepts with examples and the math that supports why these principles work. In addition to teaching raw financial concepts, this book will help you develop a planning process that you can implement and revisit as your wealth grows. You will know what to do with each dollar that comes under your leadership. This is important when trying to determine if you should tackle high-interest credit card debt or take advantage of your employer's retirement plan with a matching contribution. How do you balance short-term goals and needs while having a long-term mindset and planning for the future? I have developed what I call the Financial Order of Operations. All my team members, podcast listeners, YouTube watchers, and clients have learned about the FOO, and it has set their financial futures on an entirely new trajectory. You'll soon be like them!

By following the FOO and other principles in this book, I am confident you will take your finances to the next level without sacrificing the freedom to enjoy each moment in life and create incredible memories. All the while, you will also be quietly building a financial empire, thus creating a whole new level of abundance. What sets the FOO apart is that it is both educational and offers a plan of action that will change your outlook on building wealth.

Despite what culture, social media, snake-oil salesmen, the financial industry, and fad pushers want you to believe, here is a reality I want you to hear loud and clear: Building true wealth is quiet, patient work. It takes a strong inner voice, discipline, and time to build the foundation and reach critical mass. The outcome of having wealth can be a blast, but the path to wealth isn't lined with gold and disco balls. I want to teach you how to do the quiet, patient work that leads to your more beautiful tomorrow. If you're willing to commit for the long haul, train your Financial Mutant Mindset, and stop being distracted by get-rich-quick schemes, you will change your financial future beyond your wildest dreams. Here's the simple truth: Wealth creation is surprisingly simple and only requires mastering and implementing some important basic strategies. Big results can start with small and simple beginnings.

Simple is great, but it's far from easy. Staying consistent and disciplined, taking action with confidence, and deferring a small portion of today's money for the future may be simple, but the journey can be challenging.

This book is your guide through the madness and your invitation to start taking small steps today—steps that will fundamentally change your financial life. Here are a few data points that should both scare and motivate you along the journey:

- The average annual savings rate in the US over the last sixty years is 8.86 percent of citizens' net income.[1] This is one-third of what we have found actually creates success and is the reason so many of our peers live paycheck to paycheck. It's safe to say America has a serious savings problem.

- 20.93 percent is the average interest rate on credit cards,[2] and the majority of Americans carry a credit card monthly balance.
- 57 percent of Americans are unable to cover a $1,000 emergency.[3]
- 80 percent of millionaires are the first in their family to reach the highly coveted million-dollar goal.[4] (Don't act too shocked. You will be part of this number in the near future.)
- 77 percent to 95 percent of your wealth will likely come from the growth of your assets, not the face value of what you invested. Compounding growth is the driving force behind your Army of Dollars. We want your money to work even harder than you do! The average 401(k) balance is $112,572. However, great savers skew the data: the median 401(k) balance is just $27,376.[5]
- Those closer to retirement aren't doing much better. The median 401(k) balance at age 55–64 is just $71,168.[6]

The Younger You Start, the Less You Need to Save to Be a Millionaire

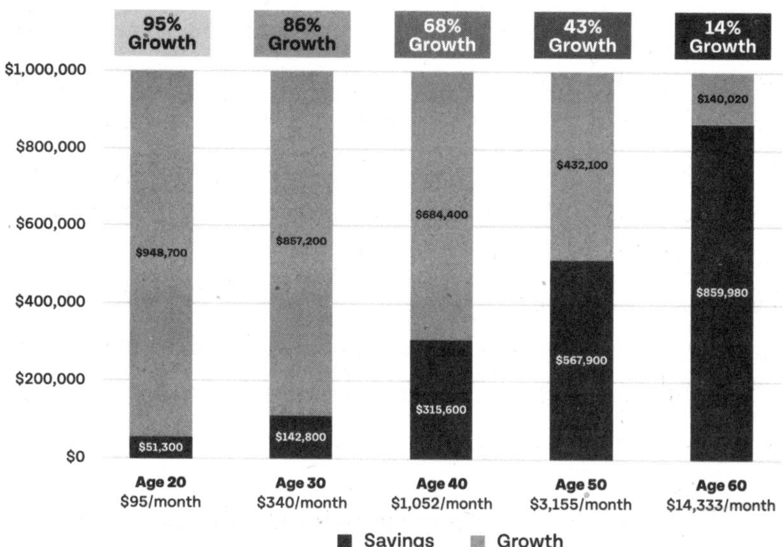

Assumed rate of return is 10% at age 20, decreasing 0.1% each year, reaching a terminal return of 5.5% at age 65.

These are just some of the statistics Americans are facing.

Before you begin practicing the strategies I've shared in this book, it's important to understand the influences, conflicts, and basic problems that have contributed to our broken personal finance system in the United States. Here are five important facts every future millionaire must recognize to be successful.

1. Many Americans Do Not Have a Foundational Knowledge of Finance

Money is universal. You need money to feed yourself, provide shelter, and buy clothes. Although money is all around us, not many people are financially literate enough to make smart money decisions. The internet can be a great financial resource if you know where to look, but there are countless websites and apps that would rather get in your wallet than improve your financial well-being. Financial literacy is rarely taught in schools, and being highly educated does not mean you learned sound money skills.

2. Everyone Who Works in Finance Has a Conflict of Interest

Even if every man, woman, and child learned basic financial literacy, that foundational education might not be enough to help them plan for their financial futures. Many of the current powers benefiting from the public's ignorance—those working in finance—likely don't want the truth in our education system since it would jeopardize their livelihoods. Financial literacy comes up in public policy or education conversations from time to time. One proposed solution for this gap in education is holding financial corporations responsible for educating the masses. Can you imagine what would happen if we let credit card companies educate and inform 18-year-olds about credit cards?

Everyone who works in finance (your banker, insurance agent, and advisor) has conflicts of interest. Even I have a conflict of interest to overcome as a fee-only fiduciary financial advisor. The more money I manage for clients, the larger the fees I earn. As you can imagine, this can be a sticky issue, for example, if a client wishes to take a large portion of the assets I manage to pay off their mortgage. I try to protect my clients' long-term well-being—even if it costs me fee earnings in the present. Fortunately, my clients understand (as will you) that I am very transparent with my thoughts on handling debt—including paying down your mortgage early. When I am transparent with my clients, and when they do their research to generate an educated point of view, our collaboration helps to overcome the inherent conflict of interest. Putting my clients' success first also makes *them* better investors and wealth builders.

3. The Media Cares About Your Eyes and Ears, Not Your Wallet

It's hard for me to watch the morning news with my kids in the room. Giving us the heebie-jeebies is the media's way of keeping us glued to the TV, radio, internet, and newspaper. The news media has an old saying: "If it bleeds, it leads." Our friends in the media learned long ago that fear, crisis, conflict, and negativity heavily influence our instincts as human beings. This fear-based method keeps us tuning in day after day.

Speaking of conflicts of interest, have you ever thought about how the media outlets you consume get paid? Almost all sources of media (including news stations, local papers, financial outlets, and radio stations) rely heavily upon advertising dollars. The more eyes and ears they can attract, the higher the price they can charge for advertising. Big advertisers (auto industry, macro brewers, medical/pharmaceutical, and financial companies) gain influence from the volume of advertising they purchase. This cycle creates a system where it's impossible to avoid abuse and bias that tends to blur the truth.

Thus, you are more likely to see ads for financial services you may not need or that are not in your best interest. Technology is quickly disrupting the old players of media and finance, but you still need to dig deep to find reputable and available resources. So, since we want to make it easy for you, we included our Wealth Multiplier, a net worth statement, and budgeting worksheet in the appendix and at MoneyGuy.com/MillionaireDownloads.

4. Innovation and Technology Are Ushering in Exciting New Opportunities

Enough with the negatives; you get enough of those every day. Here is my big, bold, audacious statement to get you excited about the future as you start the process of becoming a Financial Mutant: **There has never been a better time in history to maximize and build wealth!**

Think about all the changes and opportunities we have experienced over the last two or three decades. Once upon a time, and not so long ago, you had to go through a broker to invest in stocks, bonds, or the financial markets. That gatekeeper had a limited list of options and charged a pretty penny for their services. You could choose between individual stocks, bonds, or mutual funds. Mutual funds were all actively managed and had internal expenses and commissions that required you to make a 3–6 percent profit simply to recover all the money you lost to fees.

Innovation, competition, and technology have turned the entire system upside down. Traditional brokers, traders, and wholesalers are wondering if their jobs will exist in the coming decade. We now have investment options that allow you to buy an index of the largest US companies. It is entirely free, with zero commissions or ongoing costs.

The world is much smaller now that information flows freely through the internet and new media. Speaking of new media, you now have sources of information and education that allow you to research and solve just about any problem you might face. Is the battery in your car key fob not working? You're only a YouTube search away from a step-by-step tutorial showing you how to replace the battery yourself.

It's exciting to think of all the upcoming innovations and changes that will continue to power the growth and financial opportunities of the future. Things are not slowing down. Instead, they are rapidly accelerating. We might be as blown away by the technology of 10 years into the future as someone time traveling from 1800 would be by the technology and innovation of today.

This predictable growth in technology is called the "law of accelerating returns."[7] Here's an example to show how it works: Think about how much technology and innovation have grown from 2000 to today. We wear supercomputers on our wrists that monitor our health, call our friends, deliver and receive messages, and play music. Was this even imaginable in 2000? Did you know that your smartphone can perform computational functions 120,000,000 times faster than the technology that landed the Apollo 13 mission on the moon? Innovations will continue to grow exponentially.

Despite the momentum around us, we ourselves tend to be linear thinkers. We default to counting like this: 1, 2, 3, 4, 5, 6, and so on. We should be thinking—and calculating—exponentially instead, like this: 2; 4; 16; 256; 65,536; and so on. It's difficult to imagine the drastic rate of growth and innovation for the same reason it's challenging to save a little bit today for a more extraordinary tomorrow.

However, if you can train your mind to think exponentially, you'll become more excited for your future and a much better wealth builder. The plan is straightforward: Invest a small portion of what you earn today and benefit from an exponentially bigger reward later. When in doubt, ask yourself, *What small decision today will maximize this moment and move me closer to my more beautiful tomorrow?*

5. You Need a Road Map

It's time to buckle up and start our journey! In this book, you'll learn to harness the power of simple, smart financial decisions that go beyond common sense and maximize how hard your Army of Dollars will work for you. Your money should work harder than you do.

Do you have an Army of Dollars? Yes! I want you to change your perspective when you think about a single dollar bill. While individual bills may be seemingly insignificant, each dollar should be used efficiently and serve a purpose. As you add more dollars to your army, they go from small and inconsequential to incredibly powerful. When appropriately invested, your dollars will work harder than you can with your hands, back, and brain. Forget working just to pay the bills. Ultimately, your ability to save and smartly deploy enough money will lead you to financial independence. Not only will your money work for you twenty-four hours a day, but you will have earned the freedom to move through life motivated by personal goals and plans. Imagine living life on your terms. It won't matter if you're sleeping, on vacation, or cross-country skiing because your money is always working for you. You spend your time doing what you want, when you want, and how you want. Now that's true independence.

This book is your system and plan of action, created to help you navigate all the significant financial decisions that come your way. There is a better way to do money. This action plan will make prospering easier, so you do not have to gain wisdom through personal mistakes. This book will walk you through the common major financial decisions most of us face. Each chapter will equip you with the knowledge and mindset to overcome obstacles. You will learn to know when you are being deceived and, ultimately, how to become the best version of your Financial Mutant self.

If you're reading this book, you are *on your way* to becoming a millionaire and achieving the financial goals you've been dreaming about. Instead of loading you up with jargon and complicated formulas, I'm about to change your life with a simple, actionable, and proven system to guide your wealth-building journey. The FOO will become your lifelong go-to system for every dollar you own from here on out. The steps are sequential and progressive—they build on each other—and can apply to anyone, no matter how much or little wealth they currently have. With the FOO, no matter where you are in your wealth-building process, you'll feel better equipped to manage and maximize your money.

Understanding your relationship with money and what drives your financial decisions is an important step toward achieving a healthy relationship with money. Download homework at MoneyGuy.com/MillionaireDownloads to start uncovering your money "why." Abundance is wealth combined with purpose.

Learn the FOO, respect the FOO, and follow the FOO—and you'll always know what to do.

PART 1

The Basics

CHAPTER 1

Respect the FOO and Ground Rules

How good are you at math? Can you solve this?

$$(2 \times 4 \div 2)^2 \times 2 \div 8 - (1 + 3)$$

If you came up with zero, then you likely remember the acronym for "Please Excuse My Dear Aunt Sally!" Our grade school math teachers taught us the catchy phrase to remember PEMDAS, the correct order to solve math problems: parentheses first, then exponents, multiplication and division, and, finally, addition and subtraction.

I love that math has rules—a set order of operations—to help you navigate and confirm your calculation is correct. So much of personal finance is mathematical! Decades of assisting successful individuals as they navigate their financial decision-making have taught me there is a clear Financial Order of Operations (FOO). Following the FOO ensures every dollar is appropriately allocated to set you on a surefire path to building wealth. The FOO consists of these nine steps:

1. Cover your highest deductible.
2. Max-out your employer match.
3. Pay off high-interest debt.
4. Build emergency reserves.

5. Max-out tax-free growth with Roth and HSA contributions.
6. Max-out retirement options.
7. Leverage hyper-accumulation.
8. Prepay future expenses.
9. Prepay low-interest debt.

This is a big list, but this book lays out these steps in an easy-to-follow system. Before we go deep into each of these steps, however, we need to adopt the proper mindset and accept some financial ground rules. If you obey these ground rules, you will be financially successful in the long run. If you disobey these rules, you'll experience a much higher likelihood of failure. These aren't my rules, by the way. These are universal principles I've seen at work when it comes to money and personal finances. I'm just here to shine a light on these rules so you can avoid the traps and pitfalls that inevitably arise when you don't know to watch for them. These ground rules will apply no matter where you are in your Financial Order of Operations. And to properly leverage them, you will need to become what I call a Financial Mutant. Hear me out.

You Will Become a Financial Mutant

Most people are horrible with their money. Admit it—you know it's true. You might even be one of the people who are. A friend of mine said this phrase rang true for me: "The system you have is perfectly designed to get you the results you're getting." Because most people generally lack an understanding of financial basics, they drift through their lives hoping it all turns out okay. It's probably not going so well for them. Rudderless drifting through financial management leads to bad money habits that can be very hard to break. Bad financial habits can compound, too.

Because there is general confusion about personal finances—and ample proof that only a few people really know what they're doing—you must admit you might need a change in perspective. A new mindset. Some new ideas and habits. A new paradigm or two to reorient your financial understanding. A reset on the path to your better financial future. You need to *transform* your thinking and behaviors.

You need to develop a Financial Mutant Mindset.

I want to turn you into a Financial Mutant who can operate and build wealth outside the typical distractions and failures of the general public. This superpower mutation will not occur through a spider bite or radiation exposure. It will come from foundational financial knowledge that, once learned, is too powerful to ignore. This knowledge will change you and awaken you to what is genuinely financially significant. Keeping up with the Joneses and hyperconsumerism will become a thing of your past. As a Financial Mutant, your money will go further, and you will become a wealth builder. You can develop good habits that put you squarely in the camp of creating wealth by stacking up small incremental decisions that are pushing you closer to your more beautiful tomorrow.

You Might Be a Financial Mutant If . . .

1. You always stack the maximum number of discounts (coupon codes, credit card rewards, and shopping portals) when shopping online or in store with apps, going to the movies, or eating at restaurants.
2. You know that splitting a salad at a restaurant is a #ValueHack.
3. You know the best month to buy appliances and seasonal clothes.
4. To save money, you re-gift items that don't work for you.
5. You ask grandparents to help fund 529 college-savings plans for kiddos instead of buying toys they'll play with maybe once.
6. You gladly wait in line for twenty minutes at the Costco gas station to save fifty cents per gallon.
7. You get excited about the opportunity of investing in a bear market rather than panicking.

8. You still live a modest Millionaire-Next-Door life even when you could easily flex, but it seems pointless.
9. At financial independence, you struggle to shift from wealth creator to consumer of the wealth you have built.
10. You watch *The Money Guy Show* live stream in its entirety on Tuesday and again on Friday.

My hope is that your transformation into a Financial Mutant will occur during the course of reading this book and completing the exercises in the pages ahead. Now that you know where you're headed, let's get to the ground rules I mentioned above. You'll need to fully understand and commit to following these before you activate the FOO.

Financial Mutant Ground Rule #1: Generosity Is Not Limited to a Single "Step" in the FOO

Giving back your time and resources to charities and other organizations and people is fundamental. If you don't have money, be generous with your talent, knowledge, and time. We should all be doing our part to make our time on this planet purposeful and fulfilling. I call this concept of intentional generosity "the Abundance Cycle." When I started *The Money Guy Show* in 2006, the sole aim was helping people make sound financial decisions. There was no catch, nor were there products to sell. In the beginning, I did not even realize that this idea would be a great way to meet potential clients. I only wanted to teach the principles, help others apply the concepts, and watch them grow their levels of success because I felt the world needed more financial education. At conferences, other advisors would express concern about giving away information for which our industry typically charged. Despite their concerns, I learned that the greater my generosity, the more significant things seemed to happen for me professionally and financially. These remarkable shifts are what make up the Abundance Cycle, and its effects are not limited to *The Money Guy Show*.

We have also found that folks who are faithful and responsible with a little tend to behave accordingly with a lot. This understanding will help keep you grounded as your success grows. Having big financial success can do weird things to your worldview, so it is essential to have something that keeps you grounded—generosity does this. It is also important to remember that one of the most significant indicators of happiness is feeling that you have purpose and fulfillment. Being selfless and generous consistently show up in happiness and fulfillment research as being central to a life of purpose and fulfillment.

Financial Mutant Ground Rule #2: The Savings and Investing Goal Is 20–25 Percent (If It Were Easy, Everybody Would Do It)

The baseline savings and investing rate to build your Army of Dollars is between 20 to 25 percent of your *gross* income. Yes, you heard that right: gross income before taxes and deductions. You should aspire to this goal, despite the time it may take to reach that savings rate. The sooner you start, the easier your journey to wealth will be and the less you will have to sacrifice. Own your financial future or it will own you. If you get a later start, your savings rate requirement will increase accordingly. This book will teach you the best path to reach your ideal savings destination. It is worth repeating that big results can start with small and simple beginnings, and you should consistently ask yourself, *What small decision today will maximize this moment and move me closer to my more beautiful tomorrow?*

The following table shows exactly how much of your income you could replace in retirement by investing 25 percent at different ages.

If you start investing at . . .	You can replace
20	167%
25	131%
30	102%
35	78%
40	58%
	of your income in retirement by investing 25%.

Assuming 6% annual return, 1.5% wage growth, and retiring at 65 with an 80% income replacement ratio.

Financial Mutant Ground Rule #3: Debt Is Chain-Saw Dangerous!

Like a fueled-up chain saw, debt can be a helpful tool. However, it must only be put to work after much preparation and serious caution. If misused, it can have disastrous consequences. It is a valuable but dangerous tool that demands your respect. Hearing the word "debt" should send a chill down your spine and make the hair on your arms stand up. If you are not scared while taking on more debt, then you are likely using it wrong. Always be cautious with your use of debt.

In this consumer world we live in, *debt* is the first trap you fall into when your pride and ego want more than what you can afford—especially debt for items that will not have any value in a year or two. It is a classic tale of not understanding the difference between needs versus wants, choosing instant gratification, and not respecting that compounding interest can quickly become your enemy with the predatory interest rates of consumer debt. This debt can include credit cards to cover the cost of your fun weekends out, an eighty-four-month luxury-car loan that seems "doable" now, or using "buy now, pay later" strategies to keep up with the latest fashion trends. The sad part is most of this burden will be built with small but catastrophic purchase decisions and discipline failures. Individual expenditures seem harmless, but with time and compounding interest, the hole of debt consumes your ability to build wealth and, thus, your future. Being rich is better than looking rich.

The cold reality to wealth building is this: Financial Mutants do not struggle with basic consumption discipline. If you struggle with this basic skill set, we will help you refocus your mindset, repair the damage that debt may have already created in your life, and retain the knowledge so you will never have to worry about the dangers of debt again. The tools we provide will be life changing, and you will be converted from a consumer to a wealth builder who cannot wait to share the way out with your friends, family, and co-workers.

Financial Mutant Ground Rule #4: Keep Your Investing Simple and Be Patient

We all want to be the investor who makes millions of dollars by investing at the perfect time into the perfect investment. As I described earlier, the reality of the walk toward wealth is often quiet, patient work. You are rewarded for being disciplined, investing consistently, and having the patience to allow time to build the foundation so you can reach critical mass. This is one of those key moments that you will need to make good habits easy and bad habits hard. The way you make the good habit of investing easy is by setting up an automatic monthly investment plan (Always Be Buying). Focus your energy on slashing monthly expenses and squeezing as much as you can into your monthly investment plan. The size of your monthly investment is significantly more important than where you invest at the beginning of your journey. The bad habit we will want to make difficult is outsmarting yourself, chasing the latest and greatest investment that turns out to be a bust. This behavior not only wastes your important investment dollars, but it squanders the most valuable resource that you have: your time. We live in the greatest time to be an investor, and it is easy to minimize the bad habit of chasing investment distractions. To be successful, it is as simple as buying an investment that represents our ever-expanding global economy. Instead of attempting to beat the market's performance, why not just match and ride the performance of the growing market? Welcome to the wonderful world of index investing.

What Is an Index Fund?

Index funds will change your financial life. In many ways they are too good to be true. They outperform all but a handful of active managers, they are adored by the greatest investors in history (Warren Buffett, Jack Bogle, Brian Preston—seeing if you are awake, but in all seriousness, they are my largest personal holdings), their low fees make them almost free, and there are diverse index funds for most markets, sectors, and even conservative bonds. As you can imagine, the rise and success of these investments has turned the financial world upside down. You will save yourself tremendous heartache, precious time, and mental calories otherwise spent on where or how to invest. Let's jump into how to harness this incredible power.

Index investing is when you buy an investment that follows the ups and downs of a broad market index, for example, the S&P 500. S&P 500 index funds track the largest 500 companies in the United States. By buying an index fund, you get to own a piece of all those companies without having to pick and choose which ones to buy. You also save money on fees and taxes because you don't have to pay someone to manage your fund or trade stocks often. Index investing is based on the idea that over the long term, the market as a whole will do better than the majority of actively managed funds. Index investing can also lower risk because you're not putting all your eggs in one basket. You are spreading your money across many different industries and sectors. Here are additional details on the reasons we love index investing:

- **Index funds outperform actively managed funds.** Over the long term, index funds typically beat active funds 80 percent or more of the time.[1]
- **Index funds cost less than active funds.** The average expense ratio for actively managed equity mutual funds is over 10 times the average expense ratio of index equity mutual funds.[2]
- **Index funds are more tax efficient.** Actively managed funds have higher turnover because investments are constantly being added or dropped, which means they are less tax efficient.

Fishing for the Big Score (Individual Stocks and Crypto)

Most of us have heard this phrase: "Give a man a fish, and you feed him for a day. Teach a man to fish, and you feed him for a lifetime."

If I am teaching you to fish for dollars, what would be the most effective way to build your wealth and fish for the big score: casting with a rod and reel or using nets like the ones commercial fishers use?

To fully answer this question, I first need to help you understand the difference between investing (wealth building) and speculating (gambling). Investing is a long-term process with a very high probability of success. Speculating is usually a shorter-term decision in which you are hoping to hit the big one or the long shot.

Fishing for sport is similar to speculative investing. It can be fun, especially if you land the big score, but more often than not, it ends with exaggerated fishing stories of the big one that got away. In many ways, we all experience this when a friend, family member, or media report brags about an incredible success story with investing in individual stocks and whatever is trending on social media. With fishing, you never hear about the days your friends don't catch any fish or catch fish too small to keep. It's also probable your friends rarely share their investing losses; nobody wants to hear about the losers. Even if you find the unicorn investment, you will likely not make the perfect purchase; even if you do, you will likely sell out after you double or triple your money (and who would blame you?). This process is much more fun to daydream about than to use in building the foundation of your financial empire. Speculating should not be your first investment. You should never risk more than you are willing to lose when considering this risky behavior. As our long-term *Money Guy Show* friend and audience member Charles says, "Speculating is what you do with vacation money, not with eatin' money."

Fishing for Your Life

Now let's talk about the appropriate way to build wealth through investing. Going back to my fishing example—if you were fishing like you and your family's well-being depended on it, you would use nets, not a rod and reel. Fishing with nets would significantly increase your chance of catching enough fish to feed your family and even provide a potential long-term income source. Investing is no different. It is important to cast a wide net that increases your likelihood of success when you start investing. Index funds will be your wide nets that will fish for and create financial success. Leave the fish stories for your friends and family that do not understand proper wealth building. Financial Mutants fish with the biggest nets.

What Is an Index Target Retirement Fund?

Index funds are powerful wealth-building tools, but we need to know what index funds to buy and how to diversify your index funds over the years. You want to have a different investment strategy at 65 than you originally set up at 25. We will want to go beyond investing in equity (stock market) index funds to minimize risk and volatility as you approach retirement. Fortunately, a solution exists with index target retirement funds. Target retirement funds are designed to do much of this heavy lifting automatically by rebalancing (adjusting the mix of risky investments versus conservative/safe investments) over time as your needs and goals change. They invest aggressively while you are younger and decades away from your financial goal. Over time, they become more and more conservative as you approach retirement. This adjustment over time is called a "glidepath." Here are a few examples to help explain the investment:

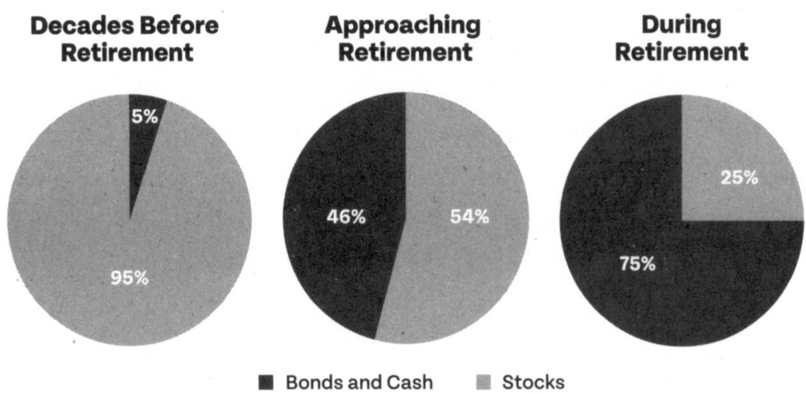

Target retirement funds come in two varieties: managed and index. For all the reasons we have already described, we prefer index target retirement funds. The index variety are significantly cheaper than their managed peers.

These are the leading providers of index target retirement funds:

- Fidelity Investments and their Freedom Index Funds
- Charles Schwab and their Target Index Funds
- Vanguard and their Target Retirement Funds

These funds make the good habit of investing especially easy by automating all of the implementation of investing for you, including asset allocation, minimizing cost and taxes, and adjusting to your changing investment needs as you grow older and approach your financial goals. They also help make the bad habit of emotional trading from fear or greed hard because those decisions are handled at the fund level. This powerful wealth-building tool lets you get a well-diversified portfolio in a single investment. To keep you on the path of wealth creation without being distracted by the numerous products and opinions on where to invest, you only need to answer two simple questions:

1. How much can you invest?
2. When will you need the money to pay for your goals?

If you can answer those two simple questions, you can invest in an index target retirement fund. Index target retirement funds may be available in your employer retirement plan, Roth IRA, Health Savings Account (HSA), and even your taxable brokerage account. Welcome to the simple and inevitable path to investment wealth!

Financial Mutant Ground Rule #5: Be Wise About Housing and Home Purchases

As long as you are renting or paying off a mortgage, housing will be one of your most significant monthly expenses. Mortgages are generally the largest debt Americans will ever owe. Thus, it is important to measure twice and cut once on all major housing-related decisions. Our guidelines suggest keeping your total housing expenditures—including rent (if you are a renter) and PITI (principal, interest, taxes, insurance)—at 25 percent or less of your gross income. This is to protect you from being house rich but life poor. Managing how much you spend on housing will also help keep your total debt payments under control. I would not want your total monthly budget for all debt to exceed 35 percent of your gross income. With many having student loan debt, credit cards, and vehicle loans, any margin left by keeping housing expenses down can be absorbed in other lifestyle expenses and debt.

If you live in a major city, that percentage may seem laughable. It is okay to exceed the 25 percent guideline if you must. Still, you will need to find that excess from somewhere else in your monthly budgeted expenses. For example, if you live within a city, you may use public transportation instead of owning a vehicle. The savings from not being responsible for fuel, maintenance, and car payments can help tremendously. However, please do not take the easy way out and assume it is okay to exceed 25 percent without considering creative options to get under this threshold. Below are a few options to reduce housing expenses:

- Living with roommates
- Renting out a portion of your home
- Increasing your income through a gig economy job or side hustle

Where Does a House Down Payment Fit into FOO?

I give you tons of latitude on your first home purchase and the required down payment. I surveyed my firm's financial planners (who are all CFP®- and/or CPA-credentialed advisors), and the majority put down less than 5 percent on their first home purchase. When we surveyed our clients in our annual wealth survey, 70 percent put down less than 20 percent on their first home, and 26 percent put down less than 5 percent. I consider this one of those dirty little financial secrets! The vast majority of advisors, financial pundits, and the general public do not put down the traditional 20 percent on their first home purchase. Saving 3–5 percent for a house down payment is much more manageable. It can be built into your monthly housing budget or even FOO Step 4: Build emergency reserves. The 20 percent down payment exception is only for first-time home purchases. The goal is to build equity in your first home purchase and easily be able to put 20 percent down on all future home purchases and upgrades.

Financial Mutant Ground Rule #6: You Only Get This Life

I primarily talk about money in this book, but please do not lose perspective on the importance of enjoying each stage of life. You can cross a line that takes you from being an excellent money master to a miserable miser. There is a delicate balance between wealth of money and wealth of time. When we are young, we are wealthy with time, but unfortunately, most of us are poor in money. As we age and find success, the tables get turned on us Financial Mutants. Financially, we become much wealthier with our money, but with each passing day we make a withdrawal out of our limited bank of time. What's below is some wisdom I've picked up along the way and seen in my clients' lives, too. Take it or leave it—it's up to you. Just know that the ground rule still applies, so you need to ensure you're not prioritizing wealth over actually living. There is more to wealth than money, and wasting time can be more expensive than wasting money.

- Focus on memories over stuff.
  - Stuff breaks and disappoints over time.
  - Memories actually blossom and improve over time.
- Don't be in such a hurry that you miss a year (or a decade).
  - In your twenties: Yes, you are broke, but so is everyone else. Embrace your energy and ability to tolerate anything. For instance, in your twenties, traveling on the cheap is completely reasonable (hostels and shared hotel rooms). As we grow older, we all tend to become more high maintenance.

Take advantage of the flexibility and low expectations in your twenties.

- In your thirties: The messy middle, often with kids in the picture, can be frustrating and challenging, but man, those precious years disappear quickly.
- In your forties: Don't let the job keep you from your "why." Create intentional space for people and hobbies you enjoy.
- In your fifties: Breathe deep and be nostalgic. Then, go do more and enjoy your life.
- In your sixties: Don't keep running up the score when you've already won the game. Keeping wealth can be as important as building wealth at this stage. It's okay to transition from saver to spender.

Do not underestimate the power of your inner voice. Suppose you do not have a purpose or believe in an optimistic future for yourself. In that case, you could be creating an unnecessary obstacle and limitation on all aspects of your life. Without purpose and optimism, no amount of money will bring you a fulfilling life. Money is a tool, not a goal. So, take control of this life and choose to nurture all aspects of your health: physical, mental, emotional, and spiritual. In many ways abundance is more about mindset and contentment, and beyond money.

Financial Mutant Ground Rule #7: Optimism Creates Opportunity

For decades, you've likely been layered in mistruths and limiting beliefs that are now your biggest barriers to success. Forget what you learned growing up. Here is a humdinger I've heard as a financial advisor: "To be wealthy I need to inherit money. I can't become rich starting from scratch." I also frequently hear this one: "If I make more money, then that means someone else is losing it as a result. Isn't it selfish to build wealth?"

I'm sure you can guess what I think about this hogwash. If you learn nothing else from this chapter, please remember this: Consistently, in all studies on millionaires, the lion's share of them (around 80 percent) have an optimistic mindset. Villains and victims are not the world changers and builders of the more beautiful tomorrow. Yes, a condescending pessimist may sound smart in casual conversations, but at the end of the day, being an optimist will make you not only wealthy but also more fun to be around. The optimists are the builders and success stories. Be a part of the positive outlook club. As you work through this book, I will share how having that optimistic outlook and inner voice will help you see the opportunity in the darkest of times. All of my biggest opportunities and learning experiences came when the light of opportunity was at its dimmest. Here are a few examples:

- My father suddenly passing away in my twenties led me to start my first business—it's amazing the clarity that can come from trauma.
- A large part of my investment wealth is built from the super-cheap investments I made during the Great Recession. Always Be Buying (ABB) no matter what the economy or media is telling you.
- The COVID-19 pandemic and working from home nudged me to finally sit down and write this book.

Let's Do This!

Okay, enough of the preamble. Are you ready to start your wealth-building journey? I know I am! This book will load you up with the real inside scoop and secrets of financial success. The herd is wrong, and you will need Financial Mutant knowledge to inoculate yourself against distractions and peer pressure. (There is a reason the Joneses are broke.) In the coming chapters, I am going to share the details of simple, automated wealth creation. This journey will be life changing, but it will be far from easy. Now is the time to decide to give the FOO a real shot. I have seen these steps bring financial security and success to people from all walks of life, and I believe they will bring abundance to your life, too.

Use the checklist that follows to determine where you are currently in the Financial Order of Operations. We encourage you to read the book cover to cover, but knowing where you are in the FOO can give you the freedom to choose your own adventure and skip ahead! You'll return to this checklist later in the book to track your progress.

FOO for You: Financial Triage

☐ **Step 1: Deductibles Covered**

Do you have the amount of your highest insurance deductible saved in a cash-equivalent account? If yes, move to Step 2.

☐ **Step 2: Employer Match**

Are you getting your full employer match? If you do not have an employer-sponsored retirement plan, or your employer doesn't offer a match, you can skip to Step 3.

When you are getting the full match, move to Step 3.

☐ **Step 3: High-Interest Debt**

Do you have any high-interest debt, such as credit card debt, consumer debt, or high-interest car loans or student loans? If no, move to Step 4.

☐ **Step 4: Emergency Reserves**

Before retirement, you need to maintain at least three to six months of expenses in an emergency fund (more depending on job security

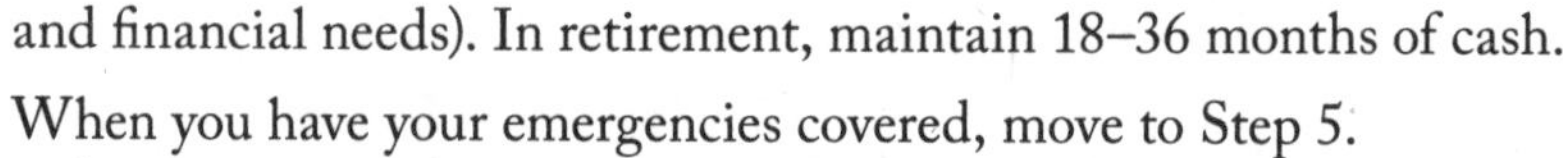

and financial needs). In retirement, maintain 18–36 months of cash. When you have your emergencies covered, move to Step 5.

☐ **Step 5: Roth IRA and HSA**

Are you maximizing both your Roth IRA and HSA, if able to contribute? If yes, move to Step 6.

☐ **Step 6: Max-Out Retirement**

Are your employer-sponsored retirement plans fully funded (maxed-out), or are contributions reaching 25% of gross income? If yes, move to Step 7.

☐ **Step 7: Hyper-Accumulation**

Optimize tax location in taxable, tax-free, and tax-deferred accounts. Make a distribution plan for retirement. You may wish to invest more if you are behind before moving on to Step 8.

☐ **Step 8: Prepaid Future Expenses**

Prepaid future expenses include saving for big vacations, your kids' college, and any other long-term financial goals, such as real estate. When you have your prepaid future expenses covered, move on to Step 9.

☐ **Step 9: Low-Interest Debt**

Are you entirely debt free, including low-interest debt like your home mortgage?

In the coming pages, we're going to cover some financial basics to establish a strong foundation for your more beautiful tomorrow. Like any project, the future outcomes of your wealth will be the result of comprehensive planning, detailed preparation, and committed execution of predetermined steps. I know you're ready to take those steps. And I'm ready to go with you. Let's do this.

CHAPTER 2

Step 1: Keep Your Financial Life Out of the Ditch (Cover Your Highest Deductible)

> Fear cuts deeper than swords.
>
> **—George R.R. Martin (*A Game of Thrones*)**

Step 1 Preview and What to Know:

Facing an emergency expense while you are broke is catastrophic. Sadly, the lion's share of bankruptcies are tied to emergencies and medical issues. The first goal of the Financial Order of Operations (FOO) is to keep you from being caught broke and making desperate decisions that you will not financially recover from. I'll teach you how to protect yourself from big emergencies with insurance and having your highest deductible covered to keep your financial life out of the ditch. I'll also help you be in a better financial position than 60 percent of your peers by taking the $200-a-Month Challenge. You'll learn to navigate the road to success by creating bumpers to absorb small financial risks while keeping yourself clear and protected from the catastrophic traps that could ruin your journey.

Don't Get Caught Broke

Have you ever been so broke that $1,000 would change your life? I have.

My broke moment came in my first year out of college. One of the best feelings in the world is making your parents proud. I could sense that my parents liked telling their friends and relatives that I graduated from the University of Georgia and landed a job at a CPA firm in Atlanta. In parental terms, they won the game; I was out of the house with a good education and gainfully employed. They could check the box on their son leaving the nest successfully. Now let's look at the reality of the situation.

My $28,000 starting salary disappeared quickly when I considered my Atlanta rent and used car payment. Don't even get me started on what auto insurance costs for a 22-year-old. It was a Mazda 626, not a Corvette. "Adulting" was kicking my butt, and I was starting to sink financially. I was not able to pay off my credit card bill monthly. Credit card debt is no-go territory since it is essentially weaponizing the most potent financial tool (compound interest) against you.

I still remember calling my father and asking to borrow $300 because I was broke and couldn't make the math work that month. I could sense his disappointment through the phone. My request brought light to the fact that the narrative of my success was more fiction than reality. I try to always remember how I felt on that call and use that memory to turn an adverse life event into the rocket fuel that drives success. I promised myself that I would make whatever changes necessary to ensure that I never made another "disappointment" call again. That $300 failure was a priceless life lesson because it humbled me and made me recognize how important each dollar is in this journey.

The first goal of the Financial Order of Operations is to cover your highest insurance deductible to ensure you do not get caught broke.

Why? When you are broke, you make desperate decisions that can haunt you. The first crutch of desperation is to use debt to bridge your emergency. The easy solution is to use a credit card. Credit cards charge predatory interest rates, and they take your net worth backward by building up debt that, at some point, you will have to pay back (plus interest). It will be hard work to get back to zero, and as you claw to pay back that debt, you have smothered your ability to focus on your actual goal of building wealth and wasted precious time. If credit cards weren't scary enough, other industries are built to take advantage of folks who get into scary situations (pawn shops, payday loans, and title lenders, just to name a few).

Every January, Bankrate releases the percentage of Americans that cannot come up with $1,000 to cover an emergency. Unfortunately, you can pretty much set your watch to the number coming in at around 60 percent.[1] The cost of even the most basic of needs or emergencies would derail the average American. This vulnerability takes away their ability to think about and react rationally to emergencies.

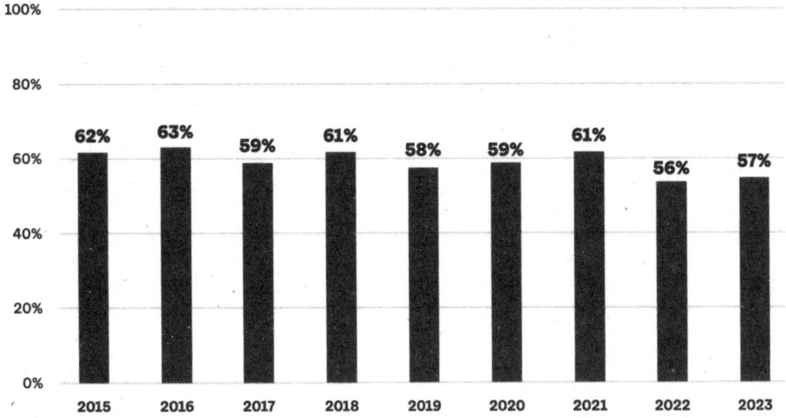

How to Be in Better Financial Shape than 60 Percent of Americans

The $1,000 of savings stat for Americans is so devastating that I want to take a few minutes so that anyone who is in that broke moment can know that there is a path forward. It will start with small decisions that when layered on top of other small decisions will create tremendous change. The first part of this redemption is to take the $200-a-Month Challenge.

The $200-a-Month Challenge

Right now head to MoneyGuy.com/MillionaireDownloads and download our $200 Challenge Checklist. This valuable resource is designed to help you uncover an extra $100–$200 a month of cash flow without taking on additional hours at the office or starting a new side hustle. These are all opportunities built off of lowering the prices of services and items you already use in your everyday life and by squeezing your daily habits to identify the unnecessary wants versus critical needs. Here are a few examples of potential cost-saving areas:

- **Ungrateful service providers.** Unfortunately there are quite a few of your service providers that have designed businesses that would rather have new customers at lower prices than keep loyal existing customers happy. In order to ensure you are not being taken for granted, you will need to remind current providers of your value and even shop new vendors to save quite a few bucks. Some of the common ungrateful service providers include:
    - Auto insurance. There is a reason these companies can have tag lines like "A fifteen-minute call could save you 15 percent or more."
    - Homeowners insurance. See above—same industry that rewards new customers over loyal existing customers.

- › Utilities. In quite a few states, utilities are deregulated. This allows you to shop different providers for electricity and natural gas.
- › Mobile phone and internet providers. In this modern world without traditional cords, ensure you keep your providers appreciative of your business.
- › Gym memberships. Use it or lose it! If you're not using your gym membership—or any other type of subscription—it's time to cut them from your monthly expenses.

- **Subscriptions.** I cut the cable cord so that I could lose my $110 monthly bill, but somehow what started as a money-savings blessing has turned into a curse. Instead of one monthly bill I, like many of us, now subscribe to multiple streaming platforms (Netflix, Disney+, Apple TV, Amazon Prime, Hulu, Sling TV, and YouTube TV). Trim this list down and reap immediate monthly savings.
- **Weekly cash flow leaks.** Cash flow leaks arise from the attitude that money is burning a hole in your pocket. A big part of my childhood was hearing my parents say, "He/she spends money like it is burning a hole in their pocket!" This applies to spending on the little extras of life that we buy out of convenience or comfort versus being a necessity.
  - › Coffee shops, juice bars, and eating out. I know we pick on the latte effect because most folks screw up the big decisions (housing and car payments) so much that these little mistakes carry a much larger grace threshold. However, this section is for those on the journey to making sure they have at least $1,000 at a minimum and hopefully on the path to having their deductibles covered. When digging yourself out of a hole, no expense is too small to review and stack as an opportunity to get back above ground and turn from a

consumer to a creator. Don't amplify bad consumption decisions by paying for expensive and fee-laden delivery services. Remember the saying that should echo in your inner voice, "What small decision today will maximize this moment and move me closer to my more beautiful tomorrow?"

› Groceries. Set a goal to audit your pantry. How much of it comprises junk food that you can take a break from for a few months, and how many items are you rebuying because you forgot that you already had a backup waiting in the pantry? Either way, a bit of austerity and discipline can cut hundreds out of the monthly budget. The Doritos savings alone could make this a fruitful and potentially healthier lifestyle opportunity.

To close out the $200 challenge, there is one more step to ensure that this is an exercise that leads to a better financial result. From the day that you download our checklist, I want you to set a 30-day reminder to review how much of your monthly cash flow savings have turned into increased cash reserves or increases to your monthly investments. It is one thing to do the exercise. It is something exponentially more powerful if this leads to you going deeper into the Financial Order of Operations to accelerate your ultimate financial success.

Avoiding the Broke Emergencies

You often hear that variety is the spice of life. That is great when the "spice" consists of positive events such as travel and trying all of the restaurants in your area, but we also know life is going to throw lots of unexpected negative events at you, too. You need a plan so that when the unexpected happens, you do not turn a short-term problem into a long-term tragedy.

- **Major financial emergencies**
  - Car accident that totals your vehicle
  - Damage to your primary residence (fire, water, hail, etc.)
  - Accident or illness that requires extended medical care
  - You become disabled for a period of time and are unable to work
- **Minor financial emergencies**
  - Drop your iPhone in the toilet
  - An appliance breaks
  - Flat tire or other auto repair
  - You get sick and need to see a doctor

While these emergencies are not anticipated, it is important to be financially prepared to handle them.

A Mindset of Preparation

Would you pay $1,500 per year to protect yourself from something that only has a 0.25 percent chance of occurring? With those odds your answer is likely no.

Would your $400,000 house catching fire be financially devastating and catastrophic? Of course it could be! It could ruin your financial life. Would you be willing to pay $1,500 per year to ensure your $400,000 house is insured even though there is only a 0.25 percent chance it catches fire?[2] Amazing how a bit of context now makes that $1,500 seem like a deal.

Fortunately, we can buy insurance to cover every one of the major financial emergencies I listed previously. These insurance premiums can be annoying to pay, but they are an important tool in your wealth-building journey. We need to have a mindset of preparation that builds savings and enough cash on hand to cover the annual premiums and required insurance deductibles.

What Is an Insurance Deductible?

An insurance deductible is the amount of money you are required to pay before an insurer pays out a claim.

This concept of buying protection from large financial risk has been around since the 1600s when ship owners were looking to protect themselves from financial ruin.[3] By pooling the risk with others who also desire to protect their finances, you turn the small but devastating risk into a manageable insurance policy. We obviously cannot control whether a horrible accident or emergency will happen to us, but we have the ability to buy financial protection from these events. This behavior of buying large protection with a small annual payment also pays respect to the first concept of wealth creation: "discipline" (more on this in Step 3: High-Interest Debt). The discipline to mitigate devastation will serve you well in the long term.

The First Step

Step 1 of the FOO—Cover Your Highest Deductible—is designed to make sure you have enough money to cover minor financial emergencies and to cover the money you will need if a major financial emergency comes your way. This first step will not be enough to make you feel safe or comfortable, but it will go a long way toward mitigating potential financial disaster. To get an understanding of what your risks are and the insurance available, you do have a few action steps to complete. First, you will start by working through the process of calculating the highest of your insurance deductibles. You'll find the deductible on your policy's declaration page, which is a summary from the insurance company of protections provided, and it also includes what is required of you, including your annual premium and insurance deductibles.

Consider Insurance to Cover Major Financial Emergencies

- Health insurance—health and medical emergencies
- Disability insurance—disability or loss of income
- Auto insurance—auto accidents or theft
- Homeowners or renters policy—damage or loss of property
- Life insurance—income for your family if you die prematurely
- Umbrella coverage—liability protection above auto and homeowners policies

The goal here is to have enough savings in reserve to cover the highest insurance deductible. When you do this, you will also have a bit more margin to make it through those minor financial emergencies. We need to have enough of a protective coating and margin for error so that the momentum you are building throughout the wealth-building process is not lost. If you do dip into those reserves for minor emergencies, do it with caution. We never know when we will have the big expenses, so make sure if you do touch those savings that you work hard to quickly replace that money. To use those funds you need the mindset that, like debt, you are handling a very dangerous tool. Let's face it: if your reserves fail to cover your emergency then your next resource is likely debt, so this fear and laser focus is completely reasonable with the stakes so high. There is a timer counting down in the background, and the time left is kept a secret—you never know when the next emergency will strike.

How High Should Your Deductible Be?

As your deductibles go up, your premiums go down. Choosing an appropriate deductible is important even if you have your largest deductible covered. If you are younger and an expensive medical emergency is unlikely, you may be able to tolerate a higher health insurance deductible than someone who is older or in poor health. Here are a few pros and cons of carrying high deductibles.

How High Should Your Deductibles Be?

Benefits of High Deductibles	Drawbacks of High Deductibles
Premiums will be lower.	Many expenses will be completely out of pocket until you reach your deductible.
Those who rarely use their insurance plan will likely save money.	If you need to use your plan more than expected, it will cost more than a lower deductible plan.
If you have a High-Deductible Health Plan (HDHP), you may qualify for a Health Savings Account (HSA).	You may not seek medical care when you should if you must pay for it yourself.

FOO Step 1 Homework–Cover Your Highest Deductible

Please do not overlook the importance of this step. It is easy to say, "Why should I research all of my deductibles when I could just make sure I have $3,000 in the bank and then move on?" The problem is, you have not done the work to determine what your risk actually is. Cutting corners on Step 1 could create a false sense of security. The last thing you want to do is build the cornerstone of your financial empire on sand. We need you to be rock solid! Let's get through the basics and build a strong foundation before we get into the sizzle of getting your money to work and grow for you.

In order to complete FOO Step 1, not only do you need to have a clear understanding of all of your insurance deductibles, you need to make sure that you have enough in cash to cover the *largest* of those deductibles. It will not keep you out of the ditch if you have $500 in reserve to cover your auto deductible but you end up with a $5,000 medical bill where your deductible makes you responsible for the first $3,000 of that cost. If, however, you have $3,000 in reserve to cover your health deductible but you have an auto accident, that $500 is already there waiting for you. Taking it a step further, even if you incur an expense that you are not insured against (e.g., dropping your phone in the toilet), those deductible dollars you have in reserve can keep you out of the ditch and prevent you from reaching for that credit card. Compounding interest on credit card debt digs you further into the ditch. Don't let emergency expenses compounded by credit card interest set you back.

The major deductibles to research and compile include health, automobile, homeowners, disability, and renters policies required to protect your household and prioritize what amount you need to save in order to be able to move on to the next step. Since we know we will have the protection of the policies for any catastrophic issues, we need to make sure you have that insurance deductible liquid and available in case an unforeseen need arises. It's worth noting that when you reach Step 4, Emergency Reserves, you will need to account for extra medical expenses beyond your deductible (co-insurance and out-of-pocket maximum).

Complete the $200-a-Month Challenge at MoneyGuy.com/MillionaireDownloads to free up extra cash flow in your budget and jump-start your progress toward covering your highest deductible and finishing up Step 1. Use the suggestions to help you spot areas where you may be able to cut expenses and save more money!

CHAPTER 3

Step 2: Love That Free Money (Max-Out Your Employer Match)

> I don't care how much money you have, free stuff is always a good thing.
>
> **—Queen Latifah**

Step 2 Preview and What to Know:

There is a shortcut to wealth and financial independence—FREE MONEY! Don't ignore the tool that can accelerate building the foundation of your financial empire: employer matches and contributions. Learn the not-so-secret way 80 percent of millionaires reach millionaire status—company 401(k) plans. Demystify employer-sponsored retirement plans and set yourself up for the success of compounding growth so you can multiply your money 88x.

Some of my favorite memories of the appreciation of "free" include the live studio audience's reactions to "Oprah's Favorite Things" episodes. What was the special component that led to such unbridled excitement and pandemonium? Absolutely everything Oprah spoke about on these episodes, the audience would receive for free. Did they really care that much about T-shirt bedsheets or Oprah's favorite bamboo pajamas?! Likely not, but the price was right, and the event perfectly captured the power of "free."

This raw excitement for free stuff can influence our behavior, and it is not limited to Oprah's studio audience. Think of how awkwardly folks dance at sporting events to receive a T-shirt that they will likely use to paint or garden in. If we have such a big reaction to these small free opportunities, how do we react when we are presented with much larger opportunities such as the free money your company's retirement plan accumulates every year from your employer's match? The data shows we don't tend to be as excited about this type of free, affirming how irrational humans are when it comes to financial decision-making:

- One in three workers, 34 percent, aren't contributing enough to get the full match from their employer, according to Vanguard's review of over five million participants.[1]
- Wells Fargo reviewed their plans (four million workers in more than 5,000 plans) and found a disturbing percentage of participants not saving enough to get the full match:[2]
  - Twenty-five percent of boomers
  - Thirty-one percent of Gen Xers
  - Thirty-seven percent of millennials

How are employees so disconnected from the value of free money that they don't have the "Oprah reaction" to it landing in their retirement accounts? When I lead retirement plan presentations, I often point out that no one sitting in the room would walk by a table of "free" $20 bills without taking one. Yet so many of our friends, family, and peers are leaving thousands of dollars on the table in their employer-sponsored retirement plans.

To put it in different terms, whereas contributing a portion of your monthly salary might mean giving up a few weeks (or less) of pay each year, that same contribution could provide *years* of income in retirement in the long run. The following chart shows how much income getting the match could provide in retirement.

Don't Miss the Match!

How much retirement income missing the match could cost you:

Employer Match	*Weeks of Pay Sacrificed per Year*	*Years of Pay Gained in Retirement*
1%	.5	1.3
2%	1.0	2.7
3%	1.6	4.0
4%	2.1	5.4
5%	2.6	6.7
6%	3.1	8.0
7%	3.6	9.4
8%	4.2	10.7
9%	4.7	12.1
10%	5.2	13.4

Including employee and employer contributions. Assuming 8% annualized return and 3% inflation, for 35 years.

The Reasons People Do Not Take Advantage of Free Employer Money

There are reasons why some people may not take advantage of free employer match in their company retirement plan even though it is a powerful wealth-building tool:

- Present bias (we covered this one last chapter, too): People tend to prioritize immediate needs (aka instant gratification) and rewards over long-term goals. This can make it difficult for them to focus on saving for retirement rather than short-term spending.
- Lack of financial literacy: Some people may not fully understand the benefits of an employer match and the long-term implications of not taking advantage of it (this book is working to erase this obstacle).
- Procrastination: People may put off signing up for their company's retirement plan because they don't have time or they don't want to take the time to research different options.
- Fear of commitment: Some people may be hesitant to commit to a long-term savings plan, even if it comes with an employer match.
- Mental accounting: People tend to separate money into different "mental accounts" and may view money going into a retirement account as "lost" money, rather than as an investment.
- Social norms: Some people may think that saving for retirement is not a priority, or that it's something that only the wealthy do, and therefore they don't feel the need to save for retirement.

These are just a few reasons and excuses, and it's important to note that each person's situation is unique. However, by understanding these psychological factors, we become more aware of the wealth-building opportunity and take steps to overcome these obstacles that may prevent them from taking advantage of an employer match. This knowledge will lead us to make the good habits of wealth-building easier and our bad financial habits harder. A system of success will power us through our emotional and behavioral limits.

"88x Over" Explained: Maximizing Compounding Interest

It's time to learn the incredible power of making your money work harder than you can with your back, hands, or brain. I call this "building your Army of Dollars" and understanding that small decisions can lead to significant change. Every dollar you invest has so much potential; if you start the process early enough, your army will grow exponentially.

Don't take my word for it. Review the "Wealth Multiplier by Age" chart on the following page. Check out our Wealth Multiplier resource in the appendix, with every age from 0 to 65, or download a copy at MoneyGuy.com/MillionaireDownloads. Notice that the one dollar a 20-year-old invests has the potential of becoming $88 by the time they reach retirement.

As soon as you understand the opportunity of what each dollar has the potential to become, you have a completely different viewpoint on the value and power of your money. This works exponentially if you apply this knowledge to your big life decisions. If a 20-year-old avoids the temptation of financing a car and instead starts the wealth-building behavior of investing every month until retirement the same amount as those $400 car payments, they could have over $4 million dollars at retirement. Do not take any dollar in your Army of Dollars for granted; each and every dollar has tremendous potential!

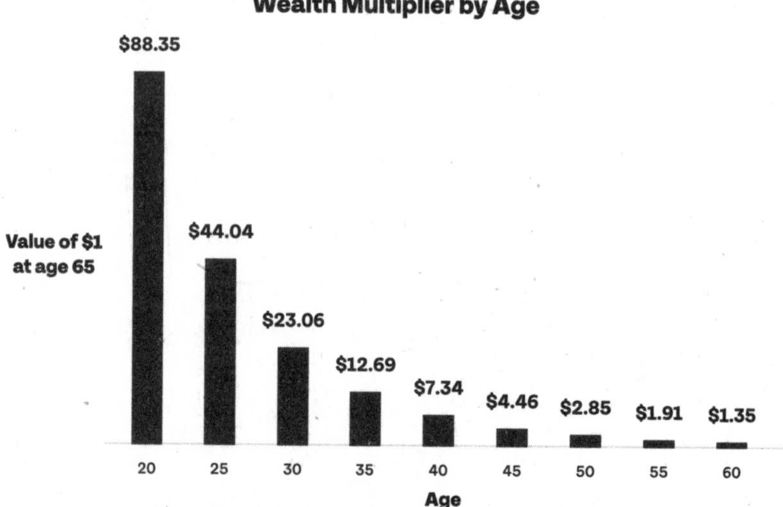

Assumed rate of return is 10% at age 20, decreasing 0.1% each year, reaching a terminal return of 5.5% at age 65.

That same dollar saved at age 20 could be even more powerful if you include the typical employer match of fifty cents on the dollar. Below, see what every one dollar saved could turn into by age 65 if invested in a 401(k) with a 50 percent employer match.

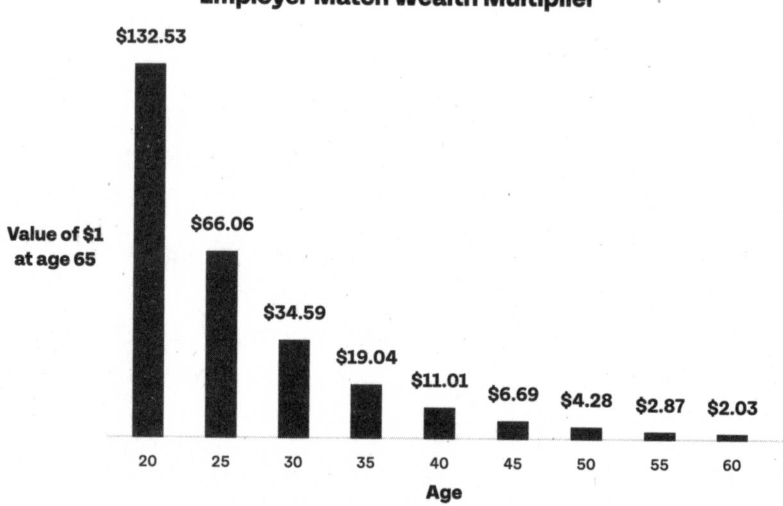

Assumed rate of return is 10% at age 20, decreasing 0.1% each year, reaching a terminal return of 5.5% at age 65.

To see what a dollar could be worth to you at your specific age, take a look at our Wealth Multiplier resource in the appendix or download your free copy at MoneyGuy.com/MillionaireDownloads.

Wealth Amplifier: Your Employer Savings Plan

Would it surprise you to learn that most millionaires credit their company 401(k) as a key component of reaching millionaire status? Ramsey Solutions conducted the largest survey of millionaires in the United States. The study confirmed what I have experienced over decades of working with successful families in the financial planning industry. Here are a few of the big takeaways:[3]

- Eight out of ten millionaires invest in their company's 401(k) plan.
- It takes an average of 28 years working, saving, and investing before hitting the $1 million mark.
- Most millionaires reached their first $1 million around age 49, proving that wealth-building is a patient journey.
- Seventy-nine percent of millionaires did not receive any inheritance.
- Thirty-one percent of millionaires have an average income of $100,000 a year or less throughout their careers, challenging common misconceptions.
- Sixty-two percent of millionaires graduated from public universities or state schools.

The first point highlights that 80 percent of millionaires are using their employer retirement plans, confirming this is an important tool in the wealth-building process. The 28 years of saving and average age of 49 are more subtle numbers, but they show that wealth is not built overnight. It is back to doing the patient and consistent work of setting up good habits to make your journey to financial success automatic. Monthly investing through your company retirement plan checks every one of those boxes to be that disciplined Financial Mutant who is walking toward inevitable wealth no matter what the world or life throws at you. I also love the empowering message of knowing that the majority of millionaires (79 percent) built their wealth without inheritance, and by attending public universities (62 percent). This means that wealth-building is an achievable goal; you just need the knowledge and system to make it happen. Respect the FOO and you will have your more beautiful tomorrow.

We conduct our own annual study, The Money Guy Wealth Survey, and have found similar results. In our survey of Abound Wealth Management clients, we found that 74 percent of our millionaire clients received nothing or less than $10,000 in an inheritance, and 67 percent attended public universities or state schools. It is remarkable how consistent these statistics are!

It makes complete sense that the majority of millionaires use the wealth-building power of retirement accounts. Retirement savings accounts include several key benefits that make them powerful tools in your journey toward financial abundance, such as consistent contributions, tax deductions, tax-deferred or tax-free growth, and "free" matching contributions. Contrast this with the fact that the median retirement account balance for those approaching retirement is only $71,168.[4] This number saddens me because I know the potential that every dollar has if it is managed well. America does not have an income problem, we have a discipline and saving problem! Too many are not focusing that inner voice to ask, "What small decision today will maximize this moment and move me closer to my more beautiful tomorrow?" Without a doubt, free money from your employer is part of that process.

Let me illustrate my point and help explain the power of compounding interest and then put an exclamation on it by adding the benefits of having an employer plan that offers free money. Once you understand this power, I hope you'll share this knowledge with everyone you know so that you can empower others to move closer to their more beautiful tomorrow. This example is going to make several unrealistic assumptions, including never receiving a pay raise, which means they never increased their savings rate, to show that even with the humblest of situations, you can achieve success with your employer's retirement plan. Let's assume the following:

- A 25-year-old saving 15 percent of their annual $40,000 salary = $500 month
- They never receive a pay raise. (This is unrealistic assumption #1!)
- They never increase their savings rate or investments. (This is unrealistic assumption #2!)
- They earn an 8.5 percent rate of return on their investment.
- They retire after 40 years of work, at age 65.
- In total, they invested $240,000 ($500/month × 480 months).

Here is the big reveal on how powerful compounding interest is for anyone who is willing to have a long-term mindset. That $240,000 of savings and investing has the potential to turn into $2 million dollars over 40 years! That's $2,019,326 for my fellow financial calculator operators. That is not a typo! Eighty-eight percent of the $2 million comes from the growth of that Army of Dollars.

Remember, this chapter is about the power of free money! By adding one additional assumption, we can take this example to an entirely new level: Their employer offers a one-dollar match for every dollar they contribute, up to 6 percent. That's $200 of additional free money each month!

Now instead of investing $500 a month, our 25-year-old is actually investing $700, thanks to that free money from their employer. Instead of $240,000 of career savings turning into $2 million, their now $336,000 of career savings ($240,000 of their savings and $96,000 of free money from their employer) actually becomes $2.8 million! What's more, 92 percent of the $2.8 million comes from compounding growth and the employer match. The incredible part of the process is that once the habit and process are set up, the journey toward wealth becomes inevitable! One small incremental decision to save and invest 15 percent of their salary is all it took to create life-changing wealth.

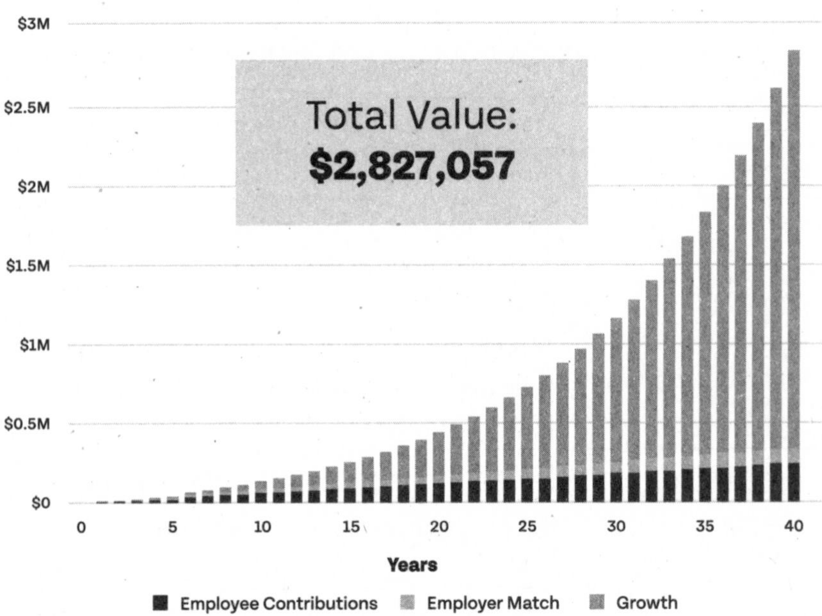

It's worth repeating that wealth creation is surprisingly simple but far from easy. Focus on saving early and consistently. It may seem challenging to lose a percentage of income each month to long-term savings, but the "little bit of today for your more beautiful tomorrow" will become exponentially larger as a result of your discipline. Vanquish the sugar high of instant gratification, and your discipline will be rewarded with financial success beyond your wildest dreams.

How Employer Retirement Plans Work

Over my career, I have advised, set up, and helped educate participants of employer-provided retirement plans—401(k), 403(b), and 457 plans.

Many employer-provided retirement accounts offer incentives and contributions to encourage participation.

Below are the most common types of employer-sponsored retirement plans:

Types of Employer-Sponsored Retirement Plans

401(k)	Most common retirement plan.
403(b)	Virtually identical to 401(k), but for nonprofits.
457	Like 401(k) plans, but for state and local government employees. Has more flexible distribution rules.
TSP	Thrift savings plans are similar to 401(k) but designed for federal employees and members of the US military.
SIMPLE IRA	IRA plan typically offered by smaller employers.
SEP IRA	IRA plan with more generous contribution limits.
Defined Benefit Plans	Now fairly rare, defined benefit pension plans offer a fixed monthly payment to employees upon retirement and require no employee contributions.
ESOP	Employee stock ownership plans give employees an interest in the company.
Profit-Sharing Plan	Retirement plan with flexible employer contributions; the company is not required to contribute if it is not profitable.

Employer contributions come in three main forms:

1. Matching dollars: Your employer matches a percentage of your contributions up to a certain limit. The most common matching formula is a 50 percent match up to 6 percent of your salary.

If your employer offers this match, they will contribute fifty cents for every dollar you contribute until your own contributions equal 6 percent of your annual salary. You are contributing 6 percent for a combined 9 percent contribution to your employer plan.

2. Non-elective contributions: Your employer funds a contribution to your account regardless of your participation.
3. Profit sharing: Your employer adds funds based on the success and growth of the company. These contributions will vary from year to year based on the profitability of your company.

The free money from your employer will likely have a vesting schedule, which means there may be time requirements on how long you must be with your employer for the benefits to become yours. There are three main vesting schedules:

1. Immediately vested: Sometimes all employer contributions are immediately vested. If your employer has a safe harbor plan, the employer contributions are always yours to keep.
2. Cliff vesting: If your plan has cliff vesting, you will be 100 percent vested after a certain period of time, such as two qualified years of service. The employer contributions to your plan go straight from 0 percent vested to 100 percent vested.
3. Graded vesting: Employer-sponsored plans with graded vesting increase over time. For example, you may be 20 percent vested after two years, 40 percent after three years, 60 percent after four years, 80 percent after five years, and 100 percent vested in the plan after six years.

What type of match or profit sharing does your employer offer, if any, and what is the vesting schedule of your retirement plan? If you aren't sure, locate your employer-sponsored retirement plan documents containing the summary plan description and annual disclosures. If you aren't sure where to find your documents, try looking in the online portal for your retirement account or ask your employer for a copy.

Why would your employer offer these contributions and give you free money? There are several reasons, but the first is that your employer wants to have a happy, healthy, and successful workforce. I know this goes against the narrative often provided by the media, but it is true. As a small business owner, I get no greater fulfillment than watching my employees achieve personal success and fulfillment in their lives. A big long-term component of that is to have a stable and prosperous financial future. The government also recognizes the benefits of having financially healthy citizens, so there are tax incentives provided to both employees and employers to save and build assets for the future. The deductibility of retirement contributions "greases the skids," encouraging the positive behavior and setup of these powerful retirement savings tools.

In addition to getting you motivated to maximize your employer's free contributions, I hope the 88x Over concept of compounding growth will have you rethink how you use every dollar in your Army of Dollars. Once your eyes have been opened to the potential of every dollar, it will make you rethink not only how often you order drinks and lattes but also the big life expenses that can completely derail your wealth journey. Those big-ticket items include what vehicle you drive and the house or apartment you live in. The goal is to build wealth and abundance, and not just look rich. Keep your goals and the "why" always front and center.

Use the checklist that follows to ensure you are effectively taking advantage of your employer match and your employer-sponsored retirement plan.

Get That Free Money

- [ ] **Determine your employer match.**
  Find out how much money your employer could contribute to your retirement account. This may be a percentage of your salary or a fixed amount.

- [ ] **Review your plan details.**
  Understand the terms and conditions of your retirement plan, such as the vesting schedule, investment options (are there index funds?), and plan fees and expenses.

- [ ] **Get the full employer match.**
  Contribute at least enough to get the full employer match. A 100 percent or 50 percent guaranteed rate of return even beats out high-interest credit card debt.

- [ ] **Contribute more to your plan.**
  After getting your full employer match and maximizing your Roth IRA and Health Savings Account (HSA), it may be time to consider increasing contributions to your 401(k). Did you get a pay raise? Increase your contributions. Be cautious about front-loading your account and crowding out some of the employer match.

- [ ] **Monitor your account.**
  Keep an eye on your investments and rebalance as necessary. Don't forget about your plan if you leave your job.

- [ ] **Get help from a professional.**
  Once your account reaches a critical mass, it may make sense to bring on a professional financial advisor.

CHAPTER 4

Step 3: The Joneses Are Broke and Miserable (Pay Off High-Interest Debt)

> The rich rule over the poor, and the borrower is servant to the lender.
>
> **—Proverbs 22:7**

Step 3 Preview and What to Know:

Turning compounding interest into your enemy is a grave mistake. You choose your relationship and how the power is harnessed for or against you. Any high-interest debt you carry is burying your financial life under the weight of punitive interest rates. This step will be your debt safety-training course. I will focus on the debts with the biggest risks of having high interest, including auto loans, credit cards, and student loans. I will reveal how debt traps are set and ways to close the traps, and dive deeper into the three ingredients to creating wealth. You'll even have the opportunity to say the Financial Mutant Debt Oath! Given that 57 percent of

Americans cannot cover a $1,000 unplanned expense,[1] the influential Jones family so many try to keep up with are likely similarly unprepared. They are focused on what each dollar can buy them today rather than the significance of each dollar for their future. This focus on consumption through instant gratification is not sustainable or productive. If only we could help them see that small decisions can lead to their more beautiful tomorrow. Financial Mutants ask an important question about every dollar in their possession: What could this dollar become if given the opportunity to grow? This one key shift of mindset—a focus on wealth building versus consumption—will change the direction of your financial life. The opportunity to grow requires understanding three key ingredients in wealth building.

Discipline, Money, and Time: The Three Ingredients of Wealth Building

The process of wealth creation is so simple but proves difficult for the majority of people. Too often, the pursuit of wealth creation is derailed by a dangerous financial tool: debt. And debt works against all three of the basic ingredients of wealth building.

- Discipline. Live on less than you make.
- Money. Be purposeful and make the margin work for you (invest).
- Time. Money multiplied by time can create exponential compounding growth. Wasting time is more expensive than wasting money.

Wealth Ingredient #1—Discipline and Deferred Gratification

To have money to invest, you will first need the discipline to save. Why be disciplined and live on less than you make when you can use debt to get instant access to whatever you want as long as you can afford the monthly payment? The YOLO mindset of renting your life by using credit cards can feel like a much easier path than owning your life by earning and waiting to get what you want, but it is not the way to build wealth. Instead, you'll need to practice discipline and deferred gratification.

Discipline is important because it helps you know your financial boundaries so you can live on less than you make. Doing so will help you save money regularly, invest it wisely, and avoid impulsive spending, which are all part of making good habits easy and bad habits hard. This is a twofer because discipline allows you to establish easy good habits such as automatic monthly investments (Always Be Buying) while creating Forced Scarcity that makes bad habits harder, given that every dollar will have a purpose. Deferred gratification is essential because it helps individuals to prioritize long-term goals over short-term wants. Wealth building requires sacrifices and hyperfocus on future goals to save and invest for your more beautiful tomorrow.

Together, discipline and deferred gratification are practices that can make saving and investing a habit, helping you build wealth over time. By focusing on long-term goals, such as retirement or buying a home, rather than short-term wants, such as shopping, eating out, or spending with reckless abandon, you'll get closer and closer to financial security. The shift in mindset will also help you overcome the short-lived pleasure of instant gratification decisions since you will now have an eye on building something that is on a different level of success. The benefits will be exponentially better for you and your loved ones.

It's important to note that wealth building is not just about financial gain; it's also about building a future marked by independence and freedom. Making small decisions now can save you from having to make big decisions later. Saving now hurts less than cutting later.

Wealth Ingredient #2—Money from Discipline Creates Savings and Margin

Money deployed into investments is your Army of Dollars that we count on to grow exponentially through compounding growth. If all of your money is too busy covering the minimum payments on your debt, you will have no money to invest. In this way, the discipline to live on less than you make is creating the money to invest, and this is essential to building wealth. In the beginning, savings rate matters more than rate of return.

Having money from your discipline creates a margin, or a buffer of savings and investments to build a financial foundation. This reserve of resources can help you to weather financial emergencies, such as job loss or unexpected expenses, without going into debt. It can also give you the flexibility to pursue opportunities, such as investing in a new business or taking a job with a lower salary, without worrying about how to make ends meet. Having money creates the benefit of flexibility as life comes at you.

By respecting this ingredient and putting these habits in place, you are able to take control of your finances, reach your financial goals, and be prepared for the future.

Wealth Ingredient #3—Time (the Most Potent Ingredient in Wealth Building)

Your Army of Dollars needs time to grow and harness the power of compounding interest. If debt delays your investing, your Army has less time to grow. Time is the most potent ingredient in the wealth-building process for several reasons:

- **Time can either be your ally or foe—you choose.** Start saving and investing early enough, and it will amplify your good financial decisions. The power of compounding growth is that the returns on your investment are building upon prior income and returns, and given enough time, this is a powerful force that will likely make up the majority of your total retirement account value. Procrastinate too long on saving and investing, and you have missed the advantage and exponential growth opportunity, pushing more of the weight of future financial needs being carried by your labor and time. The third and most detrimental choice is to take on debt and then take your sweet time to repay. This decision will delay and minimize the benefits of compounding growth while allowing the interest to layer on top of the debt and quickly diminish the light and power of wealth-building opportunities. The speed and hopelessness of the negative compounding is directly impacted by how high the interest you carelessly agreed to repay is.
- **Building wealth takes time and consistency.** Wealth requires a long-term approach and a consistent effort so your money builds upon itself over time. In the beginning, your savings and investment rate may be more about starting the behavior than meeting the desired savings rate goal. Choose today to be the moment that you start the practice of consistency.
- **Time allows space for mistakes and learning opportunities.** We all make mistakes, and no one is perfect when it comes to building wealth. Having more time allows you to learn from your mistakes, make adjustments, and fully recover.

The earlier you start, the more paths lead to success and wealth generation. If you procrastinate too long or make bad consumption decisions at the wrong time, you will find that the path to success narrows and more of the responsibility falls on a larger portion of your earnings and labor. The goal is for your Army of Dollars to do the heavy lifting so you can own your time and live your best life sooner.

The Timing of Major Purchases Is Extremely Important

It is crucial to understand how the timing of major purchases impacts your future financial success. For example, say you purchase a fancy car because the monthly payments are affordable and driving it would make you look fabulous. While this may seem like a reasonable decision based on the apparent affordability, this one decision could devastate your wealth-building journey. Let's look at the effects of buying a $73,395 Corvette at age 25 versus age 61 (surprisingly, 61 is the average age of actual Corvette purchasers). Isn't it amazing that advertising companies use beautiful twenty-somethings in their commercials? The reality is that their buyers are much older and more financially established. The commercials create an emotional response that is disconnected from reality and a perception that this is what young and successful folks aspire to be. They are also providing a wink to their older buyers that they will feel and look younger in the Corvette. Let's push through the manipulation to see how the timing of this consumption decision impacts the wealth-building process for a consumer that is led astray, even if up to this point they have been in the top 10 percent of net worth for their age group:

- For a 25-year-old who has a net worth of $59,900 (top 10 percent of their age group), the Corvette purchase would represent 123 percent of their total net worth.

- For a 61-year-old with a net worth of $2,596,800 (top 10 percent of their age group), the purchase price of that same Corvette represents only 3 percent of their total net worth.

What's most at stake in this example and others like it is *opportunity cost.* If instead of purchasing the Corvette, the 25-year-old invests the $73,395 for forty years, it would turn into $3,232,118 by retirement (growing at 9.5 percent annually). As a numbers person, I am amazed that a $73,395 decision at age 25 has the potential to exceed what, in today's dollars, would put you in the top 10 percent of wealth for sixty-somethings. Remember, time is the most scarce and valuable of the three ingredients. Act accordingly! Decisions you make today can have a big, lasting impact on your financial future. This one decision could be a seven-figure misstep. As stated earlier, we all make mistakes, but it is important to minimize the big timing and consumption mistakes.

Making smart financial choices in your younger years can give you a head start on building wealth and can set you up for a more financially secure future. Do not fall prey to our society's fixation on consumption that encourages cutting corners by using debt as a bridge so you can look cool to folks who, in reality, do not care what car you drive or what labels are on your clothes.

Now that we have helped you refocus your mindset from consumption for today to building something beautiful for the future, we can go deeper into how to understand and use debt in your financial life.

It is important to remember that "debt" is a four-letter word just like the other cuss words that your mother washed your mouth out with soap for saying. It is a shame that we do not require graduation from a debt safety class before we allow anyone to use this dangerous tool. So why even use debt if it is so bad? Even with all of my issues with debt, the majority of us will still have to make use of this dangerous financial tool.

Many of you have student loans from college, you will need a reliable vehicle to get you to your job, and you will need a mortgage to buy your first house. It is a necessary part of our financial system, and you need to learn how to use it responsibly.

How Is the Debt Trap Set?

Why is debt such a big problem? On the surface, debt appears to fix a major problem of life: a shortage of money. When you are young and out on your own for the first time, you have so many wants, but you quickly realize that you don't have enough money to buy everything. There is a siren song that claims to fix all of your money and consumer woes. I even fell into this trap myself when I could not cover my monthly expenses and minimum payments. Credit cards seemed like the easy solution.

Debt is the bridge that will turn your list of wants and desires into reality, and in the beginning, help you cover any shortfalls. All you have to do is make the minimum payment on the accruing interest. For $100–$200 a month, you can load up your broke-as-a-joke life with all of the trappings of success. This plan seems so simple because your hope is that the move is a temporary step on your path to making more money. You tell yourself that you will not only pay off your debt, but you will also make up the difference on what you should have been saving for the future with your next pay raise or promotion. This is the beginning of stacking bad habits and decisions on top of other bad decisions and habits.

In the beginning, this plan of faking it until you make it works incredibly well. Even with a modest income, you can get approved for a mortgage, financing for a nice car, and access to whatever other lifestyle purchases you want using credit cards and personal loans. The problem comes as the lifestyle continues to creep, and the debt and minimum payments continue to build in the background. Lifestyle creep is the expansion of your spending on nice cars, designer clothes, better vacations, and even upgrading your housing before you can responsibly afford to. As you build more debt to fund your lifestyle, you also start to turn the power of compounding interest against you. This time the interest payments on the debt are only getting bigger and bigger as you barely make a dent with the minimum payments, instead of saving that money and having the interest work in your favor.

Below are average monthly payments of different types of debt. Imagine if just one or two of the categories below was instead saved for retirement. Wake up before the high-interest debt bridge overwhelms you!

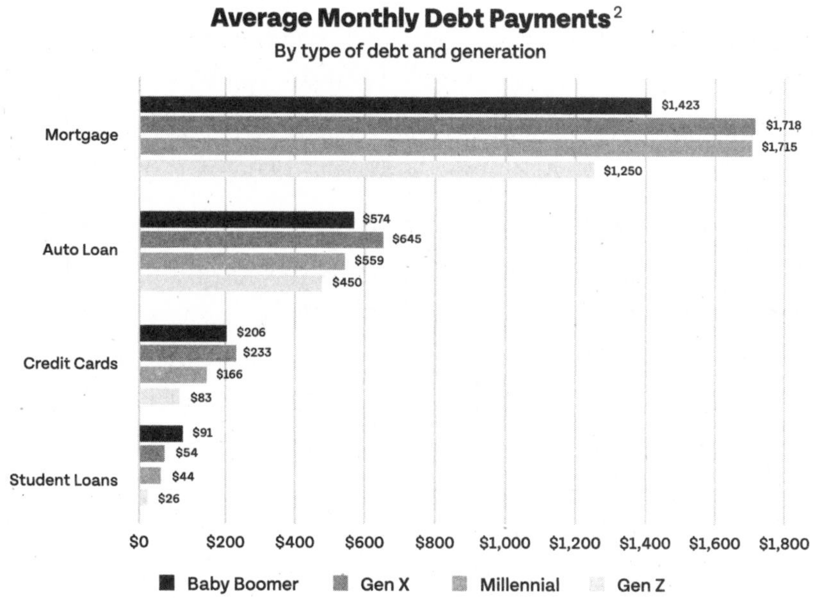

Note about the chart: student loan payments are low due to income-based plans, not due to student loan balances being low.

High Interest Debt: Know It and Vanquish It

There are three main debts that usually carry higher interest rates and undermine your long-term financial success:

1. Auto loans
2. Credit cards and consumer debt
3. Student loans

Auto Loans: Driving Toward Financial Destruction

Besides lifestyle inflation and running up credit card debt, the car you drive is a big financial trap that many people fall into. The auto industry has created a societal expectation that you should reward yourself with a vehicle after graduation or a promotion, or for the holidays. Have you noticed that the majority of auto manufacturers offer a $500–$1,000 discount to new college graduates? This graduation "gift" isn't necessarily helpful to young people, as it just reaffirms the idea that how you look is more important than building financial wealth. Here are a few additional stats to make sure you have the appropriate perspective:[3]

- $725/month is the average monthly car payment in the US for a new vehicle—$516 for used and $586 for leased.
- $1.56 trillion is the amount of outstanding auto debt in America.
- $40,851 is the amount the average American borrows for a new vehicle; $26,420 for used vehicles.
- 69 months is the average loan term for new cars; 67 months for used.

Now balance those figures with the understanding that vehicles depreciate 20 percent to 30 percent in the first year, and, according to Black Book, your vehicle will lose 60 percent of its value in five years.

Sugar High to Hangover: The Emotional Roller Coaster of Car Financing

In addition to the fast depreciation, you will find that you adapt to the new car quite quickly. The dopamine lift is short-lived, yet you are left with the financial weight of paying for the vehicle for years to come. As we shared, the average loan term for a new vehicle is 69 months. If you know cars lose 60 percent of their value in the first five years, and that most Americans are financing their cars for nearly six years, you can see how this is a recipe for financial disappointment and quicksand for long-term success.

Financial Guardrails: The 20/3/8 Rule for Car Ownership

Obviously, the auto industry is not going to help us make good financial decisions. They spend approximately $35.5 billion annually in advertising to push these money traps on us.[4] The banks are not going to protect us either; their incentive is to keep us borrowing for these financial sinkholes. It is going to fall squarely on your shoulders to understand the risk and build boundaries for yourself.

We have developed a Money Guy Rule to keep you between the guardrails financially. Remember the numbers 20/3/8 as your guide for owning safe, reliable, and affordable transportation. This will not be your path to impressing or wowing your friends and neighbors with a curb stunner. The 20/3/8 rule is function over form; think Corolla, not Land Cruiser.

Whenever you purchase an automobile, you should put at least 20 percent down. There is some flexibility in the 20 percent rule for first-time home buyers, but that is not the case with vehicles. Unlike houses, cars are a quickly depreciating asset, so putting 20 percent down is a must.

Since cars depreciate so quickly, you need to have yours paid off in three years or less. For luxury vehicles, if not paying in cash, you should pay it off within one year. If you can't do that, you can't afford the luxury vehicle!

To ensure you are buying an affordable vehicle that isn't detracting from other areas of your financial life, keep your total monthly car payments below 8 percent of your gross income. Additionally, your monthly investments—such as 401(k) and Roth IRA contributions—must be greater than your monthly car payment.

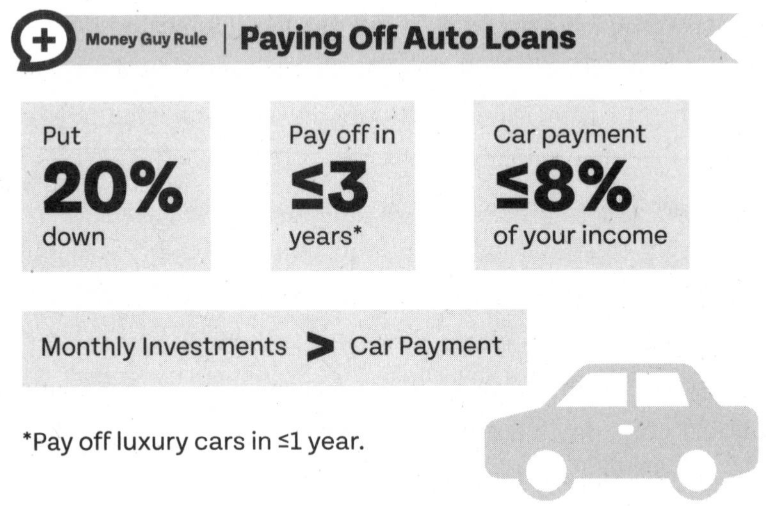

How Much Does Your Car Really Cost?

I want to insulate you from another risk that is prevalent in the auto industry and also draw attention to the importance of every dollar in your Army of Dollars. The auto industry has figured out that most of their customers are not focused on the balance sheet of their financial lives. Most are focused on their cash flow and whether they have enough to cover all of their living expenses one month at a time. This is why one of the first questions you will be asked when you walk into a car dealership is, "What is your monthly payment or what are you hoping to have your payments be?" With any answer over "$0," you have likely fallen into the trap of their financial game.

Earlier, I shared that $725 is the average monthly car payment in America. If we assumed a 6 percent car loan interest rate, you can calculate that a $725 monthly payment using my 20/3/8 rule results in a car loan of $23,831. That is well below the average car loan in America.

Assuming you put down the required 20 percent, you are buying a $29,789 vehicle.

The auto industry has figured out that if they can push out the length of your average car loan, it can result in a huge difference in how much vehicle you purchase. We know that the average car loan on new vehicle purchases has increased to 69 months, but would you be surprised to learn that they actually offer seven-year loans (84 months)? If you changed 20/3/8 to 20/7/8, that one simple adjustment (of how long you finance the vehicle) boosts the loan amount to $49,628. Changing that one variable, the amount of time you were willing to finance the car, doubled the amount available to finance.

You are probably catching on and realizing that many of your neighbors and friends with fancy cars are not half as successful as they look. They are building a shaky bridge of debt to finance their fake-it-till-you-make-it lifestyle. Unfortunately, that is not going to work out well because in addition to faking the trappings of success, they are losing the opportunity to save and invest their Army of Dollars to build financial success.

Here is a calculation to bring all of this into perspective and highlight the opportunity cost. That four additional years of $725 monthly payments would total $34,800 ($725 × 48 months). If, over those four years of payments, you were instead investing the $725 a month, you would have $41,703 at an annual 9 percent rate of return. That is bad, but here is the rest of the story that will make you sick. What if this decision was made when you were in your early thirties, and that $41,703 had the opportunity to grow for an additional 30 years and build for financial independence? That $41,703 would grow to $614,309. I almost feel guilty sharing this with you because you will forever judge those driving fancy cars, especially if it is before they have built their foundation of financial success. A fancy car purchase is a decision that should be made in Step 8 of the Financial Order of Operations (Funding Abundance Goals). Do this out of order and you are working against your accelerated journey to building financial independence and owning your time sooner.

Why Allow Any Vehicle Debt?

First, I am completely good with paying cash for your next car. That is actually the way the majority of my firm's millionaires purchase their vehicles. However, that is not always possible, especially at the beginning of your wealth-building journey. This clarification is necessary because I recognize that car debt is a disaster for your finances. So why do we allow any car financing within our Money Guy Rule? Why not buy a high-mileage used car for cash and be done with it? Because for many, reliable transportation is a necessity to make sure you make it to your initial engine of success: your JOB. I grew up in a house with a father and brother who were incredibly handy, especially at repairing and restoring classic cars. Their talent and skill made the idea of driving a high-mileage car reasonable. My father even kept a mechanic's tool bag in cars he drove (just in case).

Does that work for a mechanically challenged individual (the guy writing this book)? How do you feel about your children riding around in a vehicle that cannot be trusted to crank every time you turn the key or press the button to start?

That risk and fear is real, so I have created a process that takes into account what is reasonable but does not derail your long-term financial goals. I want to be very clear; you need to check your ego and pride. The grace and flexibility of 20/3/8 is to buy a humble and very reliable vehicle. This is not your bridge to impress your neighbors with a luxury SUV. Requiring a 20 percent down payment ensures that you are not underwater on that vehicle right after you drive it off the lot. Requiring that you pay off the car in three years protects you from devastating depreciation. That short payoff schedule of three years in conjunction with the 8 percent of your gross income limit, and the guidance that your monthly investments should exceed your monthly auto payments, ensures that you are not buying a vehicle bigger than your income justifies. I am definitely trying to keep you grounded to act your wage. Sitting on top of all this is the umbrella rule that this only applies to non-luxury vehicles. Vehicles are napalm for your financial life, and as I have shown, one bad decision could be catastrophic in your journey to building wealth. The day you start considering a BMW is the day that you better be able to pay cash.

The High Price of Convenience: Credit Cards and Consumer Debt

I still remember the tents set up on the most prominent corners on the University of Georgia campus when I was in college, where students lined up to apply for credit cards. What were these banks using to entice them into signing up, you ask? Potato chips! You cannot make this stuff up! These students were indenturing themselves to years of debt, punitive high interest, and the destruction of their long-term financial success for a $1.99 bag of Lay's potato chips. The situation has not improved that much over the past three decades. You probably still get pitched store credit cards at just about every retailer you visit, not to mention the solicitations you receive directly through the apps on your phone. Try to spot how many of your favorite brands are trying to lock you into spending more with them by signing up for their branded credit card. And for what? A few extra points toward one free meal or drink or other discount? The potato chip incentive trap has evolved and expanded.

Let's not mince words: Credit card abuse is a grave threat to your financial well-being. The raw, destructive power of punitive interest rates can shatter your dreams and destroy your long-term success. Credit card debt should be a resounding no-go! Credit cards should be treated with fear and respect, with the understanding that accounts will be paid in full each month. If you struggle with keeping credit cards paid off, it's best to avoid them altogether. This is a tool that is restricted only to Financial Mutants who pay off their balances monthly, and it does not impede them from making wise financial decisions. If you're currently carrying a balance, it's time to take drastic measures to pay off that debt immediately.

Living a balanced life becomes an impossibility when credit card debt weighs you down. To escape this disastrous situation, you must become laser focused on doing the hard work required to regain control. It starts with making sacrifices, such as no more eating out and reevaluating major cash flow elements such as the car you drive and the place you call home. However, shrinking monthly expenses is just one side of the equation. You must also find ways to boost your income through side hustles or taking on extra hours at your job. It requires self-awareness, discipline, and an unwavering commitment to knowing and respecting your limits when it comes to this dangerous financial tool.

Remember, credit card debt has the power to indenture you to the point of becoming a servant to the banks of your credit cards. The path to true financial freedom lies in breaking free from the clutches of credit card debt. It's time to reclaim control, rebuild your financial life, and ensure a secure and prosperous future. By avoiding the pitfalls of credit card debt, you will steer clear of the shackles of consumer debt. Stay on the path of liberation and own your financial future by paying off credit cards monthly. If you struggle to pay them off monthly, avoid them altogether.

Let this serve as a wake-up call—credit cards may seem convenient, but the hidden costs and potential consequences are too great to ignore. Take a stand, make informed decisions, and pave your way toward a debt-free and financially empowered future. The choice is yours, and the rewards are immeasurable. Do not build a fake life with money you do not have to impress people that do not care.

What Does Credit Card Debt Really Cost You?

I talk about the potential of your Army of Dollars through investing, but this assumes you have the margin to invest. Every day we all make small financial decisions that actually can have a very large long-term impact. Let's look at how the average American is costing their future self over $500,000 by using credit cards the wrong way.

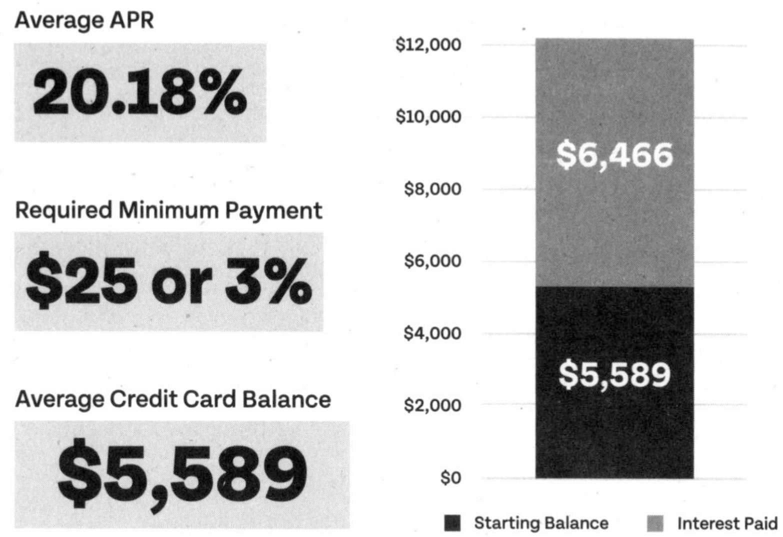

According to Experian, the national average credit card balance for American individuals is $5,589.[5] With an average interest rate of 20.18 percent,[6] it would take almost 15 years of making the minimum payments to pay off that balance (assuming you were not adding more debt to the card!). That initial $5,589 in credit card debt would cost that consumer more than double—$12,055—just because of the interest that the credit card company charged.

This is horrible because the consumer items that they had to have at the time are probably now (15 years later) wasting away in a garage or closet or have been discarded because they are broken, outdated, and outright ugly under current style standards. These were disposable lifestyle purchases that they paid almost a 100 percent premium on because of the interest expense.

What if I told you that the $6,466 of interest charges was only the tip of the iceberg when it comes to what these decisions are costing consumers?

Opportunity Cost of Credit Card Debt

An important money skill is understanding opportunity cost and the power of incremental decision-making. Small decisions have big impacts on your future. Every dollar in your Army of Dollars has the potential to either be spent, given away, or saved and invested. That "fork in the road" moment where you are deciding the fate of that individual dollar is an incremental decision. Spending the dollar now means it is gone forever and never had the opportunity to be invested and to grow. If you spent a dollar that you did not currently have access to, then you have not only spent a dollar you have but also obligated yourself to pay it back later, likely along with accumulated interest. As you can see, this can definitely change your perspective on what each dollar means to you. The opportunity cost is the calculated value of what that dollar could have become if invested instead of being spent. If you invested that $5,589 of credit card debt and $6,466 of finance charges over 15 years, it could become $38,747 (growing at 10 percent annually).

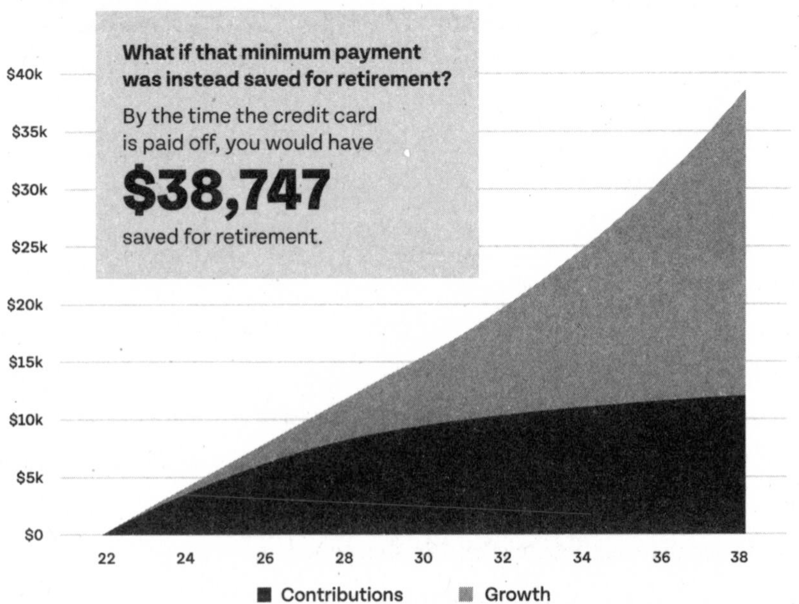

That is right, the opportunity cost of those consumer decisions can have a huge impact on your financial life. Let's go a step further and assume we let that $38,747 continue to grow until age 65 at 10 percent per year. By retirement, having made those small lifestyle discipline decisions could lead to having $570,128 in investments!

The Power of Compounding Growth

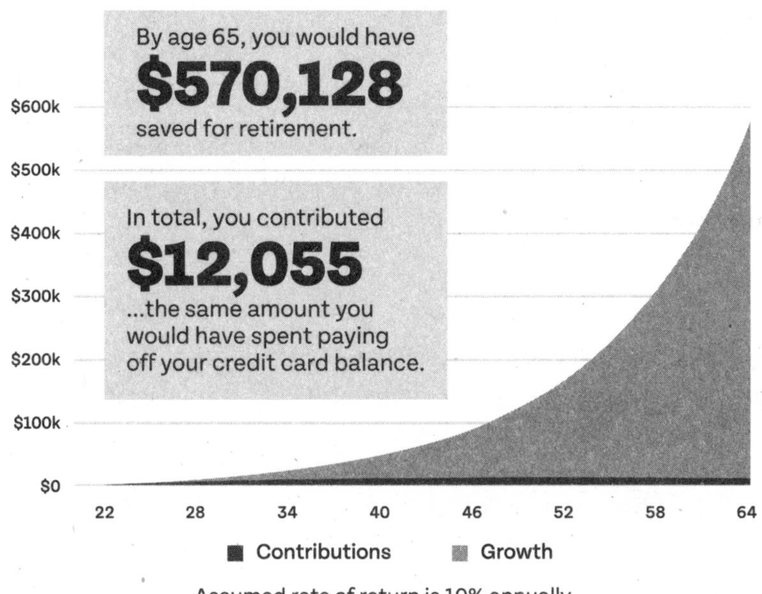

Assumed rate of return is 10% annually.

Credit Cards Are Chain-Saw Dangerous with Perkalicious Benefits (for Financial Mutants Only)

Credit card debt is horrible! However, credit card use as a financial tool can be convenient—and dare I say even beneficial. Does it surprise you to find that I have such a disgust and fear for something but still make use of it?

I use credit cards like a freshly sharpened chain saw. Chain saws are skin-crawling scary—there is a reason every haunted house in America measures their success by how many fueled-up chain saws they have built into their fear plan. While scary, chain saws are also incredibly useful at cutting trees. Similarly, credit cards, while dangerous, can be used responsibly and yield several key benefits:

- Convenience. One of the biggest advantages of using credit cards is their convenience. They are much easier than paying with cash. Credit cards are extremely convenient for both in-person and online transactions. You have the power to make purchases almost anywhere and at any time. You also can track your spending through detailed statements and easily manage your expenses online.
- Fraud protection. There are lots of bad folks trying to get into your wallet through theft, compromised websites, and scams. Credit cards provide a layer of security, as they offer fraud protection and allow you to dispute unauthorized charges.
- Price protection. Picture this: You buy the latest tech gadget that you have over-researched, and a week later, you spot it on sale at a lower price. Frustrating, right? No worries, because many credit cards offer price protection as a perk. Price protection allows you to claim a refund for the price difference if an item you purchased drops in price within a certain time frame. With credit cards offering price protection, you know you are getting the best deal. It is worth checking to see if your credit card offers this amazing benefit.
- Purchase protection (extended warranties). We've all experienced that punch to the gut when something breaks shortly after the manufacturer's warranty expires. Here is where your credit card can save the day. Many credit cards offer purchase protection that extends the manufacturer's warranty for at least another

year. This means the credit card company may reimburse you for repairs or even provide a replacement.

- Building your credit. Responsible credit card usage can boost your credit score, opening doors to numerous benefits. For instance, a solid credit score can help you qualify for lower insurance premiums, as insurers often consider your creditworthiness when determining rates. It can save you money on utility deposits, as utility companies may require smaller or no deposits for individuals with good credit. Also, when it comes to important loans and purchases, such as a mortgage or auto loan, a higher credit score can lead to better interest rates, potentially saving you thousands of dollars over the life of the loan.
- Rewards and perks. As Financial Mutants, we expect our money to go further than our peers' money, and credit cards can help make that a reality. From cash back to travel points, credit card rewards can put money back in your pocket or fund that dream vacation you've been longing for. Imagine earning cash back on everyday purchases like groceries, gas, and dining out. You will relish that you are essentially getting a discount on what you already buy. Credit cards can accumulate points you can redeem for flights, hotel stays, or upgrades, turning your travel wish list into reality. But rewards are just the tip of the iceberg. Credit cards often come packed with additional perks, such as travel insurance, airport lounge access, and even free upgrades. However, remember that all of these perks can be very expensive if you are not disciplined enough to pay the balances off in full each month. Do not get yourself in such a frenzy over these benefits that you lose focus on the danger of this tool. *Know thyself.* If you have any concern about paying them off monthly, then it is still best to avoid credit cards altogether.

Single or Multiple Credit Cards?

If you spend time reading, listening to, or watching personal finance content, you know there is an entire industry that highlights the benefits of maximizing credit card rewards and perks. There is even a guy in California who has earned a Guinness World Record title by having 1,497 credit cards in his name.[7] Give me a break! That is not worth the hassle factor of keeping up with that many obligations! It is easy to get caught up in the pursuit of funding your family vacation for free by maximizing your credit card sign-up bonuses and perks. It is important to remember that many of these financial influencers and websites get paid good money through the affiliate links funded by the banks offering the credit cards.

Simplicity is your friend, and the fewer lines of credit the better, for several reasons. If you only have a few open lines, it is less likely that a bill or payment slips through the cracks. Missing a payment can have a big impact on your financial life. You immediately start building late payment fees and interest. If the debt extends past 30 days and you have not made a payment, you run the risk of being reported to the three credit reporting agencies. This one small mistake could turn out to be a big deal since credit scores influence so much these days, including what you pay for auto insurance and if your local utility company will turn on or off your lights.

You may want to consider a one to three credit card strategy.

One-Card Minimalist

Consider a great, well-rounded cash rewards card. It is not hard to find a cash rewards card that provides 2 percent cash back on purchases with no limit. I like the simplicity of this strategy, and that you don't have to keep up with spending categories or what month you get reward boosters. An added benefit is that these cards can automatically deposit cash rewards into your brokerage account. No waiting for a check to show up and no work on your part to deposit (and not re-spend) those dollars!

Two- to Three-Card Reward Maximizer

I get it, you are a Financial Mutant, and you want to maximize opportunities, especially on purchases you will make often. Use a well-rounded cash-reward card, and then add in a card or two that heavily rewards frequent-use categories. These reward cards provide good rewards (usually between 3 and 5 percent) on key categories such as gas, restaurants, and travel.

My Credit Mistakes

I have made mistakes when it comes to credit cards and consumer debt. Learn from these mistakes:

1. **Understand what goes into your credit score.** When I purchased my first home, I thought it would be a good idea to window-dress my credit score by lowering the available credit on my one card so the mortgage company would be impressed with how small my debt footprint was. Early twenties Brian did not understand how credit scores work, obviously! This made my debt utilization percentage high and resulted in a lower credit score. It is important to understand the criteria that credit reporting agencies use to evaluate you:
    a. Payment history. How consistently you pay your bills.
    b. Credit utilization. How much debt you use compared to how much debt you have available. Lower is better!
    c. Length of history. How long you have had a credit history. It's fine to close old lines/cards, but be careful of closing your oldest line.

d. Types of credit. Revolving (like a credit card) or secured (like a mortgage)?
e. Credit inquiries. How often you are applying for new lines of credit.

35% Payment History
30% Credit Utilization
15% Length of History
10% Types of Credit
10% Credit Inquiries

2. **Avoid opening new lines of debt when buying a house.** My wife and I were so excited about our first home purchase that we decided to start furniture shopping before we had even closed on the new house. At one of the furniture stores, I was enticed to take advantage of the 10 percent savings and opened a store credit card. That hard credit inquiry cost me an additional 0.25 percent on my mortgage rate because of that one knuckleheaded decision. It also lowered my overall credit score.
3. **Store credit card discounts and perks may not be worth it (hassle factor).** In the beginning of my journey, I was so hungry to create margin and savings that I focused on decisions that had small benefits but large obligations and risk. I just shared that a 10 percent discount on a furniture purchase led to a spike in my first mortgage rate. As I have gained financial wisdom, I have learned that discounts or zero percent financing from opening store credit cards may not be worth the hassle factor. Yes, it is nice to receive a discount in the moment (present and

short-lived benefit), but it is not worth the long-term obligation of ensuring that the card is paid off monthly or maintaining the account if it is a store that you do not frequent. All it takes is one missed payment or a bill to get lost or overlooked for all of those discounts and perks to become quickly overwhelmed with late fees and interest (store credit cards typically have higher interest rates than regular credit cards). This has happened enough in my house that we have a hard rule against new store credit cards.

Financial Mutant Debt Oath

At this point, you are trying to figure out where you fall in all of this. Maybe you are in the midst of using revolving credit, and perhaps you've made a few mistakes like I have. Or you are considering getting a credit card and wonder if you trust yourself enough to make use of this very dangerous financial tool. Either way, credit card use is so dangerous that you have to be a very special type of person to do it well. Unfortunately, the majority of the public struggles with this basic self-discipline and carries a credit card balance (55 percent according to CNBC).[8]

The decision to use credit cards should not be an afterthought or taken lightly. I want you to promise yourself that if you take this step toward using credit cards as a tool, you will also take an oath that you will not, under any circumstances, fall into credit card debt. In three decades of helping successful people deal with financial decision-making, we spend zero time discussing credit card debt because it is not something financially successful people struggle with. Credit card debt is for the public that has not realized how financial success is built and does not "Respect the FOO."

At the beginning of this chapter, I said that I wished the public was subjected to a credit card debt safety course before they were granted access. Well, consider yourself a graduate of Financial Mutant training on healthy debt management. Your graduation certificate and oath are provided below.

> I, ____________________, promise to only use credit cards as a tool. I will not, under any circumstances, fall into credit card debt.
>
> X ____________________

Remember, to keep your Financial Mutant status, you will need to make sure you are paying off that high-interest debt monthly. No ifs, ands, or buts—it is a binary decision!

Student Loans—Rocket Fuel for Your Future or Long-Term Trap?

Education is a big contributing factor on my journey toward success. It has also been a part of my family's walk; my mother and grandmother were educators for their entire careers. I believe that education is the ladder out of many socio-economic situations. Attending the University of Georgia opened my eyes to so much. I met and was able to develop relationships with others from all walks of life, wealth, and backgrounds. Choosing a harder and more rigorous major (accounting) ensured I had a job before I even graduated. When I was young and inexperienced but needed clients to have confidence in my recommendations, I used additional education and designations to create that depth of knowledge and build trust. Investing in education has been some of the best money I could spend on my success. It continues to pay dividends since the majority of my business growth comes from obtaining clients who learned, applied, and grew their wealth through the educational opportunities and Abundance Cycle we offer on *The Money Guy Show.*

There is so much good that comes from education that there is tremendous public goodwill. However, the elevated status and power of education has been exploited over the last three decades. Take a moment to review these jaw-dropping facts:[9]

- About 45 million Americans have student loans.
- There is $1.76 trillion in total student loan debt as of late 2022.
- The average debt of the class of 2020 is $28,400.
- The average inflation rate for college tuition is 8 percent per year.
- Colleges have added well over 40,000 new degree or certificate programs since 2012. Universities have turned to niche degrees in fields such as casino management or peace education to attract more potential students.
- Forty-eight percent of academic programs turn out 10 or fewer graduates per year.
- Seventy-three percent of the public does not work in their field of study from college.

We have a large number of students leaving college with an extra-large helping of student loan debt. That is acceptable if there is a plan to use that education to increase your current and future income prospects and then pay down the debt. That extra earning potential should justify the student loan debt that allowed the improvement to your financial life. I am disappointed that our colleges are not helping in this uphill battle by being reasonable with annual education price increases. An 8 percent average inflation rate for college tuition is two and half times the average inflation rate of 3.22 percent.[10] Unfortunately, there are quite a few students and families who fail to understand the need to focus on return on investment (ROI) in both their degree and institution of choice. Choosing a public, private, or community college can have a massive impact on overall cost, and, while tuition costs are rising for all students, not all degrees hold the same amount of earning potential and job prospects. Many have fallen into the trap of thinking the concept of general education would be enough to create success. The state of college tuition in America is a problem, but for now, what we Financial Mutants *can* control is how we choose to engage with it.

What Is a Good Benchmark for Student Loan Debt?

How do you educate and protect yourself from overpaying for your education needs? The second habit Stephen Covey discusses in *The 7 Habits of Highly Effective People* is "Begin With the End in Mind." Before any student or family locks themselves into debt for education, they should do an analysis of why and how this will benefit them or create success in the future. **My benchmark is to not allow your total student loan debt to exceed your first full year of anticipated income.** For example, if your major is education, and you know that your anticipated salary in your first year is $35,000, then you should work hard to keep your total student loan debt below that $35,000 level. This guideline will help set boundaries and keep you focused on the level of debt that is appropriate when considering upcoming income. By keeping the total debt tied to your anticipated income, it also helps you map out a reasonable debt repayment plan that leaves enough margin to invest, save, and spend without taking on additional debt. If your debt is too big in relation to the income you will earn in your career, you run the risk of struggling to ever pay it off. You will be trapped in student loan debt.

"These College Majors Have the Hardest Time Paying Off Student Loans"[11] (highest median earnings needed for student loan repayment in first year):

- Drama and theater
- Health and physical education
- Civilization
- Ethnic studies
- Composition
- Speech
- Fine arts
- Nutrition and fitness

"These College Majors Pay Off Student Loans Easier"[12] (lowest median earnings needed for student loan repayment in first year):

- Engineering (Industrial, Electrical, Energy, Mechanical, Chemical, General, Computer)
- Nursing
- Operations and Logistics
- Computer Science
- Finance
- Economics
- Construction Services
- Special Needs Education
- Accounting and Actuarial Science

Private Versus Public College

You are free to use your money as you desire, but my goal is to make sure you understand all the implications of each choice before you make your decision. Will the additional cost of a private college benefit you over a state school or even a community college? Here are the surprising facts we found:

- Analyzing the Fortune 100 company CEOs:[13]
  - Eighty-nine percent graduated from non–Ivy League schools.
  - Forty-seven percent came from state schools.
- Our own Money Guy Wealth Survey found that 63 percent of our clients graduated from public college, 24 percent private, and 13 percent went to neither or a combination of both.

If you do go to a private college, make sure that you don't leave any money on the table. Our research shows that 89.8 percent of freshmen receive financial aid from their private colleges and universities.[14]

When to Pay Off Your Student Loan

Once you are out of college and trying to determine how to tackle student loan debt, follow the FOO. As part of the Financial Order of Operations, the answer depends on your age and specific situation. I have created a process that balances the desire to maximize the compounding interest opportunity young investors have versus being prudent and paying down their student debt as fast as possible. The last thing I want is for the Money Guy family members to drag around student loan debt even though they haven't graced a college campus in thirty years. I like having a process because it removes the emotional component of decision-making. There is a reason our wealth management firm works with so many nerdy engineers, accountants, doctors, and pilots. They love that much of my firm's interactions with clients comes through nerdy constructs and hours of pondering. Before

I share the Money Guy student loan rules, you need to understand a few important financial concepts.

When you invest, the return you receive is really made up of two "theoretical" components. The first is the "risk-free rate of return." This is basically the return you receive for simply not spending your dollars. You can think about it like putting money into a savings account. While it won't make a ton, you will earn some interest, and there really isn't any "risk" putting your money in the savings account.

The second component of your return is called the "risk premium." As you probably guessed, the "risk premium" is the return you receive above and beyond the "risk-free" rate. For example, if you invested your money in the stock market, you would expect it to make more than your savings account because of the additional "risk" you are taking. The difference between the return you receive (for example, 8 percent in the stock market) and the risk-free rate (for example, 1 percent in a savings account) is your risk premium.

All right, great. What does this have to do with student loan debt? Well, one of the assumptions we make is that the younger you are, the more risk you can afford to take. In theory, if you are taking more risk (from an investment standpoint), you should receive a higher rate of return. Then, as you age, your risk, and thus the rate of return you receive on your investments, should decrease. Because of this, we think you should compare the "risk premium" (the extra anticipated return for the additional risk taken) for your age to the interest rate on your student loan debt.

Using these assumptions, we have created a Money Guy Rule for paying off student loans:

Money Guy Rule | Paying Off Student Loans

Age	Prioritize loans if interest rates are ≥
20–29	6%*
30–39	5%*
40–49	4%*
50+	Prioritize student loans

*These statements are driven by understanding risk-free rate of return and equity risk premium.

Debt Snowball or Debt Avalanche?

Now that you know the importance of getting high-interest debt under control, let's talk about the proper way to attack paying down your outstanding balances. The question is: HOW?

First, create a detailed list of your outstanding debt (we have provided a checklist at the end of this chapter to help with this process). There are two plans of attack: Debt Snowball or Debt Avalanche.

1. **Debt Snowball**—This is the process of paying off the smallest debts first, and it's the method that Dave Ramsey recommends and has made famous. The Debt Snowball creates small victories early on because you will quickly pay off the smaller accounts. Those early victories will create momentum as you move toward paying off the larger account balances. This method nurtures the behavioral aspect of debt repayment. If you are someone who needs the wins to keep motivated, we support making use of this method.

2. **Debt Avalanche**—This method is for those analytical thinkers and planners who would prefer to pay down the highest-interest debt first. Highest-interest debt may also be some of your larger balances and could take longer to pay down than if you implemented the Debt Snowball alternative. However, this method will minimize the amount of interest paid to the banks. It will take a bit more discipline because you will not have the positive reinforcement of the wins of paying down the small debt balances first.

I support both debt payment methods and believe that it is an individual decision based on what motivates you and how your brain processes the financial world.

Closing Out the Debt Trap

There is a reason this is the longest chapter in the book. There is so much to cover to ensure you do not fall into the debt trap. Please take time to reprocess the examples and guidelines we shared, because if you can conquer and build the discipline to handle debt well, you will have a tremendous advantage over your friends and peers. To make the most of every dollar, ensure that there is a plan for every dollar in your Army of Dollars.

Use the checklist that follows to prioritize paying off your debts!

High-Interest Debt Payoff

☐ **List all high-interest debt.**

Make a list of all debts you have, including credit cards, personal loans, auto loans (if you aren't on track to pay it off in three years), student loans (that are high interest), and any other debts. Be sure to include the balance owed and interest rate for each debt.

- [ ] **Set debt payoff goals.**
  Set a goal for paying off your debts. Set specific deadlines and payoff goals. A measurable goal with a deadline is more effective. Use accelerators from the Money Guy, including the $200-a-Month Challenge (covered in Step 1: Cover Your Highest Deductible), to squeeze every dollar into your payoff plan.

- [ ] **Prioritize your debts.**
  Determine which debt to pay off first. It is financially optimal to pay off debts in order from highest interest rate to lowest interest rate (Debt Avalanche). If you know that to stay motivated you need small "wins," you could consider paying off smaller debt first, no matter what the interest rate is (Debt Snowball).

- [ ] **Track your progress.**
  How is your plan to pay off high-interest debt going? Are you paying off debts faster or slower than expected? Why? Adjust and make changes to your plan as necessary.

- [ ] **Celebrate your victories.**
  Take time to reflect on each milestone you reach in your debt repayment journey and use it as motivation to keep going.

- [ ] **Take advantage of your extra cash flow!**
  What will you be able to do without high-interest debt dragging you down? You can now move on to other goals like building a full emergency fund and contributing to a Roth IRA and Health Savings Account (HSA).

CHAPTER 5

Step 4: Rainy Day Done Right (Build Emergency Reserves)

> Cash is similar to the air you breathe; you take it for granted until underwater!

Step 4 Preview and What to Know:

You will need to go beyond covering insurance deductibles. Have you ever been caught in a storm without an umbrella, boots, or a jacket? In this step, I'll share my moment of being cash-strapped and only left with a promise and prayer never to repeat the mistake. You can learn from my storm to prepare for any financial event. While cash may be uncool, unsexy, and underperforming, it can provide tremendous peace during economic downturns and the subsequent chaos. Cash is also an important component of building your emergency preparedness kit; the appendix offers a foundational Expenses Worksheet and compares bank types to help maximize your cash reserves.

Rainy-Day Funds Need to Last Longer than a Single Storm

Cash and emergency reserves are so important that they show up in Steps 1 and 4 of the Financial Order of Operations (FOO). I also need to make it abundantly clear that cash is the lifeblood of financial success. I often say cash is similar to the air you breathe; you take it for granted until underwater! I use the analogy of the air we breathe to give you a visual image and the perspective to understand that what seems basic and easy to come by can become extremely valuable. Its value skyrockets when scarcity enters the equation. The next time you are in the ocean or a pool, go underwater and hold your breath. You will get a quick reminder of how this plentiful resource that we so often waste and take for granted becomes priceless. This is why cash gets two steps, and it also should be an indicator of how special Steps 2 and 3 are in your journey—they are important enough to interrupt the focus on building this powerful wealth necessity. In Step 1 of the FOO, we made sure you had enough money to keep your financial life out of the ditch by having, at a minimum, your deductibles covered. That focused savings goal was to protect you from the life events that can surprise you and derail your financial life if you are not prepared with enough margin in your cashflow. Covering your deductibles helps prevent single events from devastating your finances. That allowed you to graduate to Step 2 of the FOO to maximize the wealth-building opportunity of your employer matching your retirement contributions (free money). We then moved to Step 3 of the FOO to vanquish the high-interest debt that is turning the powerful force of compounding interest against you. Steps 2 and 3 were unique opportunities and risks that had to be addressed early and quickly because, if ignored, both could impact your ability to build long-term wealth. However, once those unique opportunities and risks are addressed, it is important to jump right back into building up the precious resource of cash reserves. We have now graduated to Step 4 of the FOO, and we are here to learn that we will need to go beyond your highest insurance deductible to ensure we have enough cash and liquidity to keep our financial journey moving through whatever life throws our way.

Unfortunately, financial emergencies may involve a string of events instead of one single emergency. This is why it makes sense that after covering deductibles, locking in the employer's free money, and getting those punitive interest debts under control, you should build a more complete emergency reserve. Now is the time to ensure that unforeseen events do not derail your progress:

- Lose your job = covered
- Injury that keeps you out of work for a bit = covered
- Major home issue that insurance won't cover = covered

Don't Fall into the Access-to-Cash Trap

Before I share what your emergency reserves should look like, how much to save, and how to maximize them, I need to keep you from falling into the trap of thinking you are smarter than whatever financial turmoil could be coming your way.

How do I know this is a temptation? Because I have made this huge mistake myself. I have fallen into the access-to-cash trap, too. This is an easy trap to ensnare Financial Mutants because we all desire our money to work hard and grow as fast as possible. Here are the details of my mistake so you can learn and not make the same mental error. Remember, I have been broadcasting *The Money Guy Show* since January of 2006 (embarrassingly, you can still go listen to our original episode and all of its amateur rawness). That period from the mid-2000s to the Great Recession had me feeling a false sense of security. I was so confident that I shared my strategy with the Money Guy family. Here is a summary of my well-intentioned (but horrible) advice:

You can avoid having cash reserves if you have ***access*** to enough liquid assets that all of your potential emergencies are covered.

This horrible advice can be funded and covered in several ways. The trap I fell into was having large "equity" in my primary residence. At the time, banks were offering free home equity lines of credit (HELOC). They would literally give you a checkbook and debit card that were directly linked to your HELOC. If you had an emergency, no problem, just write a check from the HELOC. Since I had over $100,000 of "equity," this falsely felt the same as having $100,000 of emergency reserves. This seemed ideal because it allowed me to keep focusing all of my extra savings and margin on adding to my investments instead of building up what I perceived as low-earning cash savings. Through the Great Recession, I learned that all of that "equity" I was counting on was only on paper. It quickly evaporated when the economy and real estate market tanked.

Access to Investments Is Also a Trap

The other trap of "access" plays out when you have taxable investment accounts. Why keep cash reserves when you have access to a large basket of investment holdings that you can easily liquidate and turn to cash? What could go wrong?

In the short term (less than five years), you can't count on withdrawing money from investments because the value could drop significantly. This locks in losses while the holdings are down significantly. Remember that equity markets go through cycles. Approximately two of every 10 years they go through recessions and even bear-market downturns (loss of greater than 20 percent). Cash and liquidity need to be readily available no matter what comes your way. Even if the value is up, you could incur a large taxable event with a capital gain if you needed access to cash.

When It Rains, It Pours, and It Is Raining Chaos

Have you ever heard the phrase "when it rains, it pours," that evolved from an old English proverb? Humans have noticed for centuries that negative events tend to happen around the same time, and negative financial events are no exception to this rule. The problem with the access-to-cash trap is that financial turmoil does not happen in isolation. I am talking about the stock market collapsing into bear territory, massive job layoffs, real estate values plummeting, and full-on recession that removes buyers from the marketplace. All of these elements often happen simultaneously or in quick succession. This is why it is impossible to rely upon the access to cash and investments as a viable emergency reserve strategy. In 2008, my business revenue was down by over 40 percent. At the same time, my house that appraised at $510,000 for the HELOC cratered to an estimated value of $273,500. This completely destroyed my emergency reserve strategy of having "access" to liquid assets.

As you can imagine, the HELOC did not stay viable during the Great Recession. Banks are allowed to freeze your HELOC balance and render your associated checkbook and debit card worthless. The same thing happens to those who are counting on selling their investments to bridge the emergency. Who wants to liquidate their account when their portfolio is down 40 percent?

Living through this downturn was a tremendous learning experience. My "access to cash" strategy was well intentioned because it sought to maximize every dollar of my army, but it turned out very shortsighted and unrealistic in the real world. Use the folly of my experience to create wisdom.

Cash Is King in an Emergency

Cash is unsexy, has a history of underperforming other investments, and if you hold too much, it loses value over time to inflation. However, it is extremely valuable in an emergency. Do not take this value for granted as you are working to build your Army of Dollars. That liquidity will provide comfort, peaceful nights of sleep, and even a clearer mind while your peers are running around trying to figure out how they will cover the basics. That additional flexibility in a period of turmoil will be priceless since you'll have the basics of life covered for an extended period of time. Listen to a guy who cut it too close to the edge in 2008 and 2009. I promised myself that if I came out on the other side, I would never get myself into that type of pinch again. I've kept that promise, and I would encourage you to build that margin and peace of mind into your financial life.

How Much Should You Have in Cash Reserves?

If I asked you how much in emergency reserves is appropriate, what would you say? The general rule of thumb is three to six months of living expenses. That is a great goal if you are just looking for general guidance, but we want to go beyond basic and find your specific need and know what moves the needle for you. What are the components that allow for the leaner three months, and what risks expand the need out to six months? The more you understand the components of your financial life, the better you will be equipped to adjust general guidelines to your specific situation.

A primary focal point is your career, your dependency on wages to cover expenses, and how long it would take to find another job were you to lose yours. If you carry lots of financial responsibility and have a number of family members who rely on you financially—or have a volatile income, like many entrepreneurs and freelancers do—you might want to err on the side of extra caution and build a bigger emergency fund.

You should have:

- **Three months of living expenses:**
  - If you are single and it would be easy to find another job at similar pay should you lose or choose to leave yours

    - If you are married and you and your spouse have comparable incomes
- **Six months of living expenses:**
    - If you are single with a very specialized vocation that makes it difficult or a lengthy process to find a new job
    - If you are married with a single income
    - If you have a special needs child or dependent or other unique life circumstance that requires additional margin

The Exception for Retirees

As you approach retirement, you will quickly realize that it is somewhat scary to know that you will soon be transitioning from saver to spender. This will do some quirky things to you mentally, but it also needs to be a sobering moment for you to realize the importance of being prepared for whatever could come your way during your retirement. Earlier, I shared that typically two out of every 10 years will have downturns, recessions, and bear markets. You will need to be able to cover the basics even in these scary times, so we suggest that retirees consider keeping 18 to 36 months' (one and one-half to three years') worth of living expenses in easy-to-access, liquid, or allocated safe reserves. This will provide valuable peace of mind and help insulate you from making a bad emotional decision when you are in the darkest of economic times. The scary periods can turn into tremendous opportunities in the long term, but you will not have the clarity to understand this in the moment without that comfortable financial cushion.

Do You Know What Your Monthly Living Expenses Are?

It sounds so easy to give the guidance of three to six months of living expenses (18 to 36 months for retirees), but there is a ton going on with that simple advice.

- Do you know what your monthly expenses are?
- Do you know which of those costs are fixed, variable, and discretionary?

This one simple exercise of building cash reserves might actually be the beginning of understanding and building a long-term cash-management plan. This will help ensure you have a plan for every dollar in your army. Tracking your expenses and creating a budget is foundational to wealth building. I completely understand that in the beginning it is a tedious process, but if done right, over time you will build the financial muscle memory and automation of investing that makes it easier. We have created a worksheet to help you work through this important step. The worksheet should make budgeting easier, supporting the goal of making good habits easy. You can't move on to Step 5 until you have mastered Step 4. In addition to helping you calculate your three to six months of cash reserves, this will highlight where your money is going. If you feel that you are not saving enough or you come up broke at the end of each month, this will help you spot the areas where you could improve and even cut back. Find the Expenses Worksheet in the appendix or download a copy at MoneyGuy.com/MillionaireDownloads.

Building reserve holdings for living expenses in an emergency falls into the commonsense category, but what about other upcoming expenses? You will want to plan ahead for any large expenses that will be coming your way in the coming months. Anything you are likely going to need cash for should go into this bucket, such as a child's future tuition, family vacations, home improvements, or a new car.

Online Banks Versus Your Local Brick-and-Mortar Bank

Now that you know how much you need, you'll want to ensure that your cash is in a secure location, ideally earning some kind of interest. Online banks can potentially pay more than 20 times what your traditional brick-and-mortar bank pays.[1] That number is correct—20 times!

How many of us would change our hairdresser, grocery store, or gas station to save 5–10 percent? Yet we are willing to stay with national banks for decades, and they only pay a fraction of what we deserve on our savings. According to Bankrate, the average adult American has used the same bank account for 16 years.[2] Our banks are taking us for granted and keeping that extra return for themselves. That is such a big difference that you cannot ignore the financial opportunity to house your cash reserves in an online savings account. You worked too hard to save those dollars to not maximize the opportunity.

Optimal Account Structures

Should you move everything into an online account right now? Well, that depends. Every individual will decide for themselves what works best. Here are the two most common structures:

- **Minimalist one-account structure via online bank.** This is for the young at heart who embrace technology to maximize the earning potential of their checking and savings accounts.

Pros	Cons
• Maximize interest earnings • Convenience of online banking and bill pay • Lower fees	• More difficult to deposit cash • Must pay attention to ATM fees since there is not a local ATM bank network • No local branch down the street for in-person banking needs • Must be comfortable with having an online-only experience

- **Two-Account Structure.** This allows the best of both worlds. You keep your traditional local brick-and-mortar bank or credit union for your day-to-day checking. You will then link that traditional checking account to your online savings account electronically. Use the local checking account to pay bills and for basic cash needs, and maximize savings in the high-yield online savings account.

Pros	Cons
• Have a local banking relationship. If you are a business owner, this could be especially important as your business grows and the need for a banking relationship expands. It also helps if you plan to get a mortgage or car loan. • Local ATM network. • Easy to deposit and withdraw cash.	• Adds a layer of complexity in transferring money between accounts. You will desire to keep as much of your money as possible working in the better-yielding account, while expenses will likely be paid from your traditional bank account. This will create the need to transfer money back and forth as income comes in and expenses pull the money out. • Creates additional financial relationships, so you will have twice as many statements and tax reporting documents.

Don't Forget the Credit Unions

If you are tired of dealing with the large brick-and-mortar banks that take your relationship for granted, see if you have any local credit unions.

In my experience, credit unions are more independent and still focused on building relationships and serving their members well.

Back in the mid-2000s, I was working with a woman who had come into a large windfall from a land sale. She had come to me for help creating a financial plan. Out of the blue, I received a call from the president of Gwinnett Federal Credit Union (now Peach State Federal Credit Union), Marshall Boutwell. Marshall was polite but did not beat around the bush. He let me know he was calling to make sure I had his member's best interests at heart because he was not going to put up with one of his members being taken advantage of. That call really impressed me because I could tell that he was trying to protect her. I have continued to be impressed with Marshall because that due diligence call led to quite a few additional phone calls, and we became quick friends. Knowing how Marshall loves his employees and members has shown me that credit unions still understand the importance of people. Unfortunately, large corporate banks lost the plot after they were restructured during the Great Recession. If you value a local branch and a personal relationship, put credit unions on your research list. You can find a local credit union at mycreditunion.gov.

Are You FDIC or NCUA Protected?

All of your banking relationships should be FDIC or NCUA protected. Here is the official summary of who and what the FDIC and NCUA are, according to their official websites:

- From FDIC.gov: "The Federal Deposit Insurance Corporation (FDIC) is an independent agency created by Congress to maintain stability and public confidence in the nation's financial system. To accomplish this mission, the FDIC insures deposits;

examines and supervises financial institutions for safety, soundness, and consumer protection; makes large and complex financial institutions resolvable; and manages receiverships."

- From NCUA.gov: "The National Credit Union Administration, commonly referred to as NCUA, is an independent agency of the United States government that regulates, charters, and supervises federal Credit Unions. NCUA also operates and manages the National Credit Union Share Insurance Fund (NCUSIF). Backed by the full faith and credit of the U.S. government, the NCUSIF insures the accounts of millions of account holders in all federal Credit Unions and the vast majority of state-chartered Credit Unions."

The FDIC was created in 1933 after the Great Depression. In the 1920s and 1930s, there were a number of banking failures. FDIC insurance protection aims to minimize that risk. Fortunately, since its creation, no depositor has lost a single penny due to bank failure. You can check that your bank, whether it is brick-and-mortar or online, is protected by using the FDIC's Bank Finder tool at FDIC.gov.*

The NCUA insures money in credit union accounts at the same level and is similar to the protection offered by FDIC. You can make sure your credit union participates in the protection through NCUA.gov.†

Be Careful of the Bait-and-Switch Game

Once you start researching the best online bank to work with, you will quickly realize that there are a number of blogs and websites that compile the best interest rates currently offered. Be careful sorting by interest

---

* The full link is as follows: https://banks.data.fdic.gov/bankfind-suite/bankfind.

† The full link is as follows: https://mapping.ncua.gov/.

rate and assuming the highest rate is the best option. Bankrate updates this list every month on their website.[3] As I write this, I am looking at this month's best rates, and the bank at the top of the list pays an attractive rate, more than my online savings accounts. Does that mean that I am about to fire my online bank and hire this new bank that obviously wants my business more? Nope!

My reasoning will save you tons of wasted time and effort. First, I have never heard of the bank at the top of the list. That makes me wonder how long they have been around, how I can know that this is going to be a consistently good bank with high rates, or if this is just a teaser rate to attract new business and within a few short months that high rate will quickly drop down, perhaps even lower than my current rate.

This is known as a bait-and-switch tactic. Banks count on the fact that folks do not change banking relationships once they are set up (remember that 16-year average I mentioned earlier). A better practice is to work with a banking brand that is consistently at the top of the interest rate list. There are quite a few good options out there, but make sure you take the time to research your needs and if there is an opportunity for this banking relationship to help with other parts of your financial life. It is good to have a plan for upcoming financial needs and to maintain relationships with providers that will show their appreciation for your business with competitive rates and good service.

FOO Step 4 Homework: Ensure You Get the Emergency Reserves Right

I have laid out all of the basics of what goes into a successful emergency reserve. Part of that is also sharing how to maximize the process. However, many of you may have never created a budget or tracked your living expenses to actually know what your monthly expenditures look like. No worries; I have created a foundational expenses worksheet that will help you compile and calculate what your monthly living expenses are, which you can find in the appendix. You can also download a copy from MoneyGuy.com/MillionaireDownloads. We break the expenses out into several categories:

- Fixed expenses are necessary expenses that are the same every month.
- Variable expenses can change from month to month, and some months they may even be zero.
- Discretionary expenses vary from month to month, and they aren't necessary to live.

Once you know how much you spend every month, you can check to make sure your emergency reserves accurately reflect that spending. It's a good idea to reevaluate your emergency fund size before major life events happen, like buying a house or having a child. If your emergency reserves fall below three to six months of fixed and variable expenses, prioritize building up your cash reserves before moving on to Step 5.

CHAPTER 6

Step 5: Tax-Free Armageddon (Max-Out Tax-Free Growth with Roth and/or HSA Contributions)

> Our new Constitution is now established, and has an appearance that promises permanency; but in this world nothing can be said to be certain, except death and taxes.
>
> **—Benjamin Franklin**

Step 5 Preview and What to Know:

Tax-free accounts are supercharged wealth builders! Setting up a Roth IRA and/or a Health Savings Account (HSA) allows you to build tax-free million-dollar wealth. There is a reason our government restricts who can contribute and how much. Take advantage of this incredible wealth-building opportunity! Step 5 lays out all the details, including an explanation of both Roth IRAs and HSAs, their benefits and limitations, and how to fund them.

In the blockbuster hit movie *Armageddon*, Bruce Willis's character is preparing to take on a suicide mission to save Earth from a gigantic asteroid set to wipe out every living creature on the planet. His character shares the requests and demands of the crew with government officials, and what is their final demand?

One more thing, none of them want to pay taxes again. Ever!

Did you catch that? Taxes are so universally despised that the ability to avoid paying them is written into one of the most successful "saving the world" movies of all-time (#23 according to IMDB).[1]

The ability to avoid paying taxes is a superpower. And there are two tax-free savings vehicles that are so powerful our government restricts who can have access to these wealth-building tools: Roth retirement accounts and HSAs.

1. **Roth retirement accounts.** These accounts allow you to save and grow assets for retirement, and the earnings and appreciation are not taxed. That means when you are retired and go to draw the money from this account, it will not be taxed. This is not the case for traditional retirement accounts where money goes in pre-tax and is taxed when it is withdrawn.
2. **Health Savings Accounts.** These are triple tax-advantaged, which means that your regular income is taken from your paycheck before you pay any income taxes, it goes into the HSA where it can grow for years, and then you don't pay tax on withdrawals for qualified medical expenses.

I want to take this one step further on the excitement spectrum; review the chart that I used earlier in the first chapter to share how much you must save monthly to become a millionaire by a certain age. From ages 20 to 40, savings and investments only account for 5 percent to 23 percent of the $1 million balance. The remaining 77 percent to 95 percent of the $1 million comes from income and appreciation. If you start early enough and pay attention to our maximization strategies, there is a strong likelihood that you could become a tax-free millionaire! It is much easier to do it the Money Guy way than boarding a spaceship for what may be a one-way trip to meet an asteroid.

The Younger You Start, the Less You Need to Save to Be a Millionaire

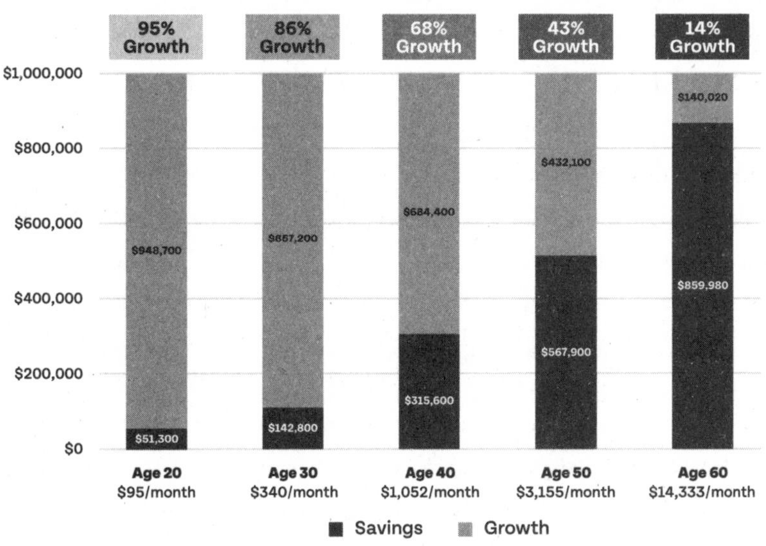

Assumed rate of return is 10% at age 20, decreasing 0.1% each year, reaching a terminal return of 5.5% at age 65.

Roth retirement accounts and HSAs are extremely powerful, and both deserve a deep dive so you can maximize each for your financial benefit.

Roth Accounts—Where Did They Come From?

A *big* thank-you to the late senator William Roth from Delaware, chairman of the Senate Finance Committee, who wanted a more flexible version of the IRA. The legislation that created this powerful tool was the Taxpayer Relief Act of 1997. Senator Roth said, "It is in the national interest both for the economy and the family that we have significant savings." What an awesome vision and legacy to create. Without a doubt, Roth accounts are a powerful tool to help families reach their financial goals.

This legislation passed with tremendous bipartisan support (90 percent in the House and 92 percent in the Senate).[2] Why would our government be so willing to forgo taxes and unleash the full power of compounding interest? Senator Roth did a good job of answering that by sharing that it was in the nation's best interest to save and plan for the future.

But there is a catch, of course. There are caps on annual contributions (we'll discuss those more in a moment). The government also limits who can participate in these plans based on income limitations (Roth IRA) and a required high-deductible health plan (HSA). The good news is: those contributions add up, and the years of layering contributions turns into legacy empire building in the long term.

Roth Retirement Accounts Superpowers and Benefits

Tax-free growth is not the only amazing benefit offered by these powerful savings vehicles. Roth savings accounts are also not subject to Required Minimum Distributions (RMDs).

What is an RMD? For many retirement assets, the government requires the money to come out starting at a certain age so they can collect taxes. When you contribute to a tax-deferred retirement account, such as a traditional IRA or 401(k), you will receive a tax deduction, and the growth of those accounts builds until you make a withdrawal. Taxes are paid on those holdings as you take withdrawals. If you reach the age of 72–75 (depending on your birth year) and have not yet made withdrawals, the government requires that you start taking mandatory distributions that increase each year based on your age and their required distribution table. Depending on the amount required, you may incur a hefty tax bill. The fact that Roth accounts do not have this RMD requirement means that they offer a long-term legacy-building opportunity since the assets continue to grow tax free throughout your lifetime.

Roth Limitations and Risk

Roth accounts are different from their traditional retirement account siblings. In the traditional tax-deferred retirement accounts, the government provides a powerful benefit with a big tax catch. The government usually allows you to take a tax deduction on the contributions (pre-tax contributions), and they grow without being taxed annually (tax-deferred growth), but when it is time to start taking distributions, the withdrawals are taxed at the higher ordinary income tax rates.

The amounts contributed to Roth accounts will not receive a current-year tax deduction and will not lower your taxes like traditional retirement contributions. The amount of the contribution is included in gross income in the year of the contribution, but future distributions and earnings are tax free.

There is a fear for many that the government's offer of tax-free growth, with a big promise that they will not tax these assets in the future, could be rescinded. This is an understandable fear with the rising national deficit, but to assume all benefits will be reversed and the government will break the promise is a bridge too far. If a change is ever made to these special accounts, there may be a high-water mark or adjustments that lock in the tax-free growth of the account up to that point.

In other words, money already in the accounts could be grandfathered in. No one knows what the future holds, but updates of the last two decades have provided more opportunities to contribute to tax-free growth accounts:

- 2010 legislation removed the $100,000 income limit on Roth conversions. This change gave birth to the Roth conversion strategy that is unofficially known as the "backdoor Roth."
- There have been legislative proposals to do away with traditional retirement contributions and push more people toward Roth accounts, another sign that Roth accounts could be here to stay.
- With the SECURE 2.0 Act of 2022, 529 (college and education savings) accounts now allow conversions to Roth accounts (with limits), and more employers are encouraged to offer Roth options in employer-sponsored retirement plans.

Roth Options and Funding Opportunities

There are two Roth funding opportunities; the first is within a Roth IRA and the second is within an employer-provided retirement plan with a Roth option. Here is another cool consideration: You can fund both at the same time. There are no restrictions on doing both as long as you meet the requirements for each (I'll explain within each structure).

Roth IRA. This is the original Roth that was part of the Taxpayer Relief Act of 1997. In 2024, you can fund $7,000. For those 50 and older, you can fund $8,000 due to an extra $1,000 annual catch-up contribution. These numbers increase every few years to account for inflation. Unlike traditional IRA contributions, the Roth IRA phaseout is based solely on income, and your eligibility is not affected by participation in your employer's retirement plan.

- Income limits for Roth IRAs in 2024:
  - Married Filing Jointly: $230,000 to $240,000
  - Single: $146,000 to $161,000

Consider Your Projected Income in Retirement

In addition to your tax rates and how they might change in the future, consider also if your income may be significantly lower in retirement.

Why this matters: If you are in a high tax bracket while you are working, but your taxable income will drop considerably in retirement, then there is a good chance you will be in a lower tax bracket in retirement. That should be included in your evaluation between Roth (tax-free growth) and traditional (deductible contribution, but taxable as ordinary income in retirement). As a simple example, if you were given the choice to save 20 percent in taxes now and pay 30 percent later or save 30 percent in taxes now and pay 20 percent later, you would obviously choose the latter.

Consider Your Expected Retirement Age

The number of years between now and when you plan to retire matters for your Roth versus traditional decision, too.

Why this matters: The younger you are and thus the further you are from retirement, the more potential your Army of Dollars has. Time is the powerful component that makes compounding growth possible. The longer you let your money grow without being reduced by taxes, fees, or spending, the bigger the tax-free growth opportunity. For young savers who are in higher-income and high-tax situations, there is still a reason for considering Roth contributions based on the tax-free growth and the possibility that tax rates will be higher in the future.

Health Savings Account

While it is easy to daydream about retiring early, a common obstacle to making that dream a reality is the concern for how to pay for healthcare in retirement. This is a legitimate fear; according to Fidelity's retiree health care cost estimate, a 65-year-old couple can now expect to spend an estimated total of $280,000 on healthcare throughout retirement.[3] If you retire before Medicare kicks in, costs could be even higher.

One of the best tools to help plan for and conquer healthcare costs is an HSA. These accounts are only available for those with high-deductible health plans (HDHPs).

For 2024, the IRS defines a high-deductible health plan as a plan with a deductible of at least $1,600 for an individual or $3,200 for a family. Since an HDHP is required to contribute to an HSA, it is important to make sure your health insurance is "HSA eligible." (Although if you or your family expect to have substantial medical costs in a given year, it may make sense to choose a great health plan with a low deductible instead of an HDHP, even if it means forgoing eligibility for an HSA.)

HSAs are an awesome (legal) tax loophole. Tax loopholes normally have negative connotations, but there is a reason the government is trying to encourage you to save and plan for your current and future healthcare needs. With the aging population of the United States, there is a big incentive for Uncle Sam to get as many citizens as possible to build their own safety nets so that the government will not be on the hook for as much of the bill. As a result, you are the beneficiary of a triple tax-advantaged opportunity! HSAs offer:

1. pre-tax contributions (meaning you reduce your taxable income with this contribution each year)
2. tax-free growth on investment earnings and appreciation
3. tax-free distributions for qualified medical expenses

In addition to these three benefits, there's a fourth honorable mention: payroll-deducted contributions to an employer-sponsored HSA are not subject to Social Security and Medicare taxes.

How to Use HSAs

You may be leaving tons of money on the table and missing a *huge* planning opportunity with how you use your HSA.

Almost all HSA users, 96 percent, do not invest their dollars; they use the HSA to pay for all current-year qualified health and medical expenses. This clearing account method allows you to take advantage of two of three benefits of HSAs. You are taking the deduction on the contribution and then using the tax-free distribution when you reimburse yourself for qualified medical expenses.

But there is a better way: investing your HSA contribution! The problem with only taking advantage of two of three tax benefits of HSAs is that you are leaving the most powerful benefit unused. If you invested your annual HSA contribution instead of using it as an annual clearing account, you would open up the opportunity of compounding growth. I know I probably sound like a broken record, but there is tremendous power in compounding over time. If you can harness the power of deferred gratification and allow time for your Army of Dollars to grow, the most incredible compounding growth and wealth building occurs.

According to the Employee Benefit Research Institute (EBRI), only 4 percent of HSAs had invested assets beyond cash.[4] This small percentage of HSA maximizers are Financial Mutants. I have been using this maximization strategy for years, and I can attest to the power you are harnessing. This strategy would be in the "top secret" folder of wealth builders.

- **Step 1.** Meet the requirements of having a HDHP and establish an HSA.
- **Step 2.** Track qualified medical expenses (keep and scan receipts for future use) but defer reimbursement so that your HSA Army of Dollars can be invested and grow.

- **Step 3.** Have enough cash reserves that you can cover all emergency needs and out-of-pocket medical expenses.
- **Step 4.** Contribute the maximum amount to your HSA for the year and immediately invest the contribution. Feel free to invest in an index target retirement fund that corresponds with the date that you would like the assets to be available. You will repeat these steps each year.

Annual Clearing Versus Fund, Hold, and Invest Comparison

Annual Clearing Account Method (96% of HSA Holders: Non-maximizers)	Fund, Hold, and Invest (4% of HSA Holders: Maximizers–the Financial Mutants)
Contribute $8,300 each year for 10 years (family maximum–disregard inflation increase)	$8,300 annual family contributions invested for 10 years earning 8% per year (on average)
Assume that each year there are $8,300 of qualified medical expenses that are paid through your HSA contributions and reimbursement	Value after 10 years (ROI of 8%) = $126,538
In 10 years, you would have contributed $83,000 to your HSA, taken $83,000 of tax deductions for the contributions, and your HSA account balance would be $0 after all expenses were reimbursed.	Reimburse yourself for the $83,000 of qualified medical expenses (tax free) at the end of the 10 years. The Health Savings Account still has $43,538 of money that is growing and available for future expenses.

Now imagine if you follow the "fund, hold, and invest" model. Consider how big your holdings grow if you expand the time they're invested to 20 or 30 years:

- 20 years = $407,406 less $166,000 of contributions; that is $241,406 of growth.
- 30 years = $1,030,832 less $249,000 of contributions; that is $781,832 of growth.

I am losing my mind at how this illustration details the power of your Army of Dollars if you will unleash them to work as hard as you do with your back, brain, and hands.

Even if you don't have 20 to 30 years before retirement for your dollars to grow in investments, there are still added benefits to using HSAs for the over-55 crowd:

Added Benefits for the Over-55 Crowd

- Once you reach age 55 or older, you are allowed an additional $1,000 per year in "catch-up" contributions. If you have a spouse who is 55 or older, they are also eligible for the same $1,000 catch-up contribution. In 2024 this would allow a married couple 55 and over to contribute up to $10,300 each year.
- HSAs are also closet retirement funds. After age 65, you will no longer be subject to penalties for using the money for non-healthcare expenses. Therefore, taking money from the account after age 65 is no different than taking ordinary income distributions from 401(k)s or other retirement accounts.
- HSAs do not require earned income in order to contribute, which is a unique differentiator when compared to IRAs and employer-sponsored plans.
- HSAs do not have RMDs like other qualified retirement accounts—IRAs and 401(k)s.

Avoid the Tax-Free Regrets

It is important to remember that both of these savings options—Roth retirement accounts and HSAs—have annual funding restrictions. Our government is willing to provide a bit of slack in the tax system, but they are not crazy about you building an empire through tax-free growth assets. This means every dollar you can save, and as early as possible, is essential.

In the beginning, missing a thousand here or there may not seem like much, but I am here to share that it can make a tremendous difference. From my own personal experience, I have regrets. I started building Roth assets in 1998. However, in five of the 24 years I did not max-out my annual Roth IRA contributions. The years I have regrets about are from the early 2000s. I started my first company in 2002, and in those early years money was tight. I left $10,000 on the table. That may not seem like much, but the lost potential of those dollars is substantial, and I can prove it.

Over the 24 years that I have had Roth assets, I have contributed approximately $98,000. As of 2023 those assets have grown to a market value of $360,000. That $262,000 of appreciation is completely tax-free! This is the power of my Army of Dollars. This is not precise math since the contributions were made at different times and values over this period, but if you normalized contributions to $340 each month with a value of $360,000 after 24 years, you would have an annual ROI of 9.3 percent. Calculating this ROI allows me to estimate how much tax-free growth I have missed out on:

- 1999 (23 years of missed growth) on $2,000 that I underfunded my Roth = $16,842.
- 2000 (22 years of missed growth) on $1,000 that I underfunded my Roth = $7,676.

- 2001 (21 years of missed growth) on $2,000 that I underfunded my Roth = $13,994.
- 2002 (20 years of missed growth) on $2,000 that I underfunded my Roth = $12,756.
- 2003 (19 years of missed growth) on $3,000 that I underfunded my Roth = $17,441.

That $10,000 of missed Roth IRA contributions would be worth $68,709 today. The situation gets worse. That approximately $69,000 of additional Roth account value would have another seventeen years of growth before retirement. That "no big deal, I missed a little bit here and there" $10,000 of Roth contributions could have grown to become $332,000 by the time I reach age 65.

Building that more beautiful tomorrow starts with the smallest of decisions and habits. Every dollar in your Army of Dollars that you are entrusted to manage has so much potential. Use my tax-free regret to motivate you to maximize and build through deferred gratification. Your future self will be so happy with that decision!

Use the worksheet at MoneyGuy.com/MillionaireDownloads to help you maximize your HSA and Roth IRA, including details on how to maximize your Roth IRA if you have a higher income.

CHAPTER 7

Graduating from the Basics and Reaching the Boiling Point

> A watched pot never boils.
>
> —**Benjamin Franklin**

In the Financial Order of Operations (FOO) Steps 1–5, we built the foundation of your financial success.

- Step 1. Deductibles covered
- Step 2. Employer match
- Step 3. High-interest debt
- Step 4. Emergency reserves
- Step 5. Roth and HSA

For a number of you, frustration could be building under the surface on this journey toward wealth. You have covered the basics, and here I am asking you to save and invest more. You may be asking yourself, "Where is the celebration and reward?!" At what point do you get to enjoy your money?

I see it all the time in our YouTube comments section, and I even hear it from friends and family: "Tomorrow is not promised; I need to live for today!" This YOLO (You Only Live Once) mindset can destroy your opportunity to build lasting financial success. I also understand the feeling that life is too short.

My family medical background does not lean toward longevity. My father passed away at the age of 55 (I was in my mid-twenties) and my grandfather passed away at 50. All of this keeps my life clock fully centered, and I recognize the weight of the ask when I challenge you to save more. This is coming from a guy who has the perspective of being financially wealthy, but with each passing day I approach poverty with my time.

The driving factor nudging me to ask for a small portion of today for that more beautiful tomorrow is knowing how important those early years of investing are to your financial foundation and long-term success. A fifteen-to-twenty-year period that you devote toward financial discipline and investments has the potential to set you up for the rest of your life. The earlier you start, the smaller the sacrifice. Have you considered what that last statement actually means? I am asking for you to get serious about saving less than 20 percent of your life so that you can enjoy the fruit of that decision for decades and beyond. I would not ask if it was not important. This is a perfect time to discuss reaching the "boiling point" of your wealth building.

The Boiling Point

At what temperature does water boil? I was surprised that several factors can change this answer, such as altitude and atmospheric pressure, but it is widely accepted that the answer is 100 degrees Celsius and 212 degrees Fahrenheit. I started the chapter with the timeless proverb, "A watched pot never boils," meaning time seems to move slowly when watching or anticipating an action or event. You can get frustrated that the benefits of deferred gratification, living on less than you make, and having good saving/investing habits are not overtly apparent in the first decade of your wealth-building journey. Do you stay the course or give up to join your peers in consuming now versus creating wealth for later? Throughout the book, I have kept repeating that small decisions lead to significant change. You should ask yourself, *What small decision today will maximize this moment and move me closer to my more beautiful tomorrow?* That question is the perfect reminder that you should stay the course because, under the surface, there is tremendous energy building that will lead to an explosive change in your financial life. How sad would it be if you started this process and quit as your financial assets approach 98 degrees Celsius or 208 degrees Fahrenheit? This is right under the boiling point but far enough away that the energy building is not apparent.

Strategies for Staying the Course

To overcome our instinct of instant gratification over the long-term good of wealth building habits and behaviors, we need a few tips and tricks to stay the course. This will ensure we do not drop out of creating wealth right as we are approaching the boiling point.

- **Make It Easy Through Automation (Lock Down the When and How Much)**—One of my favorite career achievements is the number of folks that I have nudged into wealth by squeezing them to add a dollop more to their automatic monthly investments. Wealth building is easy if we maximize set-it-and-forget-it moments. Depending on your age and how much time you have to reach the date of financial independence, a few hundred extra a month may be all that you need, and once the funding is set up, there are no additional calories or mental horsepower required for the objective to be obtained. You are on the path to inevitable wealth as long as you continue the wealth-building behavior and do not get distracted by whatever is going on in the world. Just keep practicing "Always Be Buying!"
- **Highlight the Reward and "Why"**—Stay motivated through the silent, patient work of your assets growing to the boiling

point. I encourage you to use our free Wealth Multiplier resource from the appendix or download a copy at MoneyGuy.com/MillionaireDownloads so you can remind yourself how valuable each dollar is that you are managing. If you have an itch to stray from your savings plan, it can be helpful to use this tool to remind you exactly what that decision could cost your future self or, from an optimist's standpoint, what those dollars could become in the coming decades.

We have created an easy illustration to help you see the power of perseverance when it comes to saving and investing. Do not lose focus after the first five or even 10 years of investing. The exponential payoff comes after decades. In the beginning you will be asked why you are living this way, but after your success reaches a level that is hard to conceal, you will be asked how you got to where you are. Stay motivated and consistent, and persevere to reach your more beautiful tomorrow!

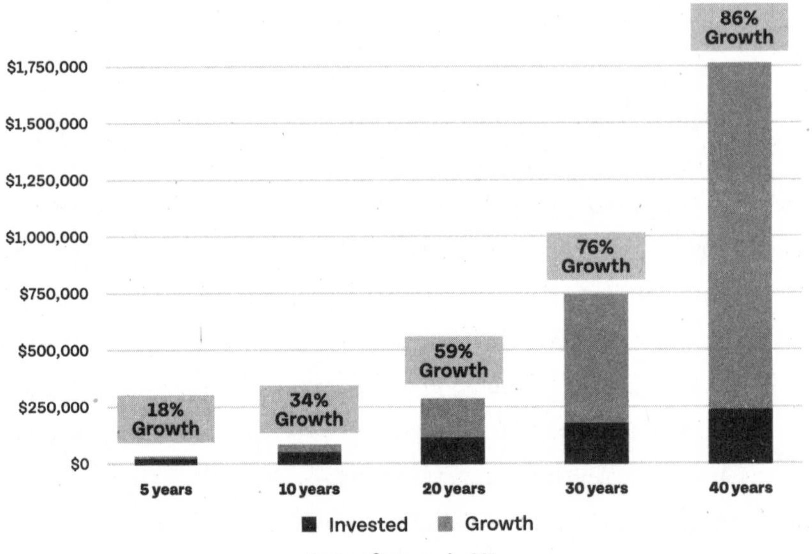

Value of Those Early Investments

To close out my pep talk on staying the course during those early years, I want you to look at "The Power of Time" chart differently. Consider this—contributing $500/month for 40 years has the potential to become $1.7 million:

- After five years of investing $500/month, your initial investment of $30,000 can potentially grow to $600,000 over an additional 35 years. Key takeaway: The first five years' contributions represent 34 percent of the potential $1.7 million.
- After 10 years of investing $500/month, your initial investment of $60,000 can potentially grow to $1 million over an additional 30 years. Key takeaway: the first 10 years' contributions represent 57 percent of the potential $1.7 million.

The exponential opportunity may not be so apparent in the first five or ten years of investing, but if you can stay the course, you will be rewarded with explosive growth and the ability to own your time and do what you want, when you want, and how you want. Be patient and give your money time to reach the boiling point.

Saving Early and Often Makes Financial Goals Easier

The benefit of starting early is that it can lower your long-term savings rate required to reach your goals. Even a small amount can have an enormous impact. Imagine two people who save the same amount every month, but at different times in their life. The first starts saving $200 a month at age 20 and stops saving altogether by age 30. The second gets a later start, and doesn't begin until age 30, but saves $200 a month consistently until age 65; the assumed rate of return for both is 9 percent. The first saver put in $24,000, and the second $84,000; but since the first saver started saving earlier, they ended up with over $300,000 more by retirement.

Early Saver

Age	Total Invested	Amount Available
20	$2,400	$2,520
25	$14,000	$19,144
30	$24,000	$42,651
35	$24,000	$66,778
40	$24,000	$104,553
45	$24,000	$163,696
50	$24,000	$256,296
55	$24,000	$401,278
60	$24,000	$628,273
65	**$24,000**	**$906,058**

Rate of return is 9% annually.

Late Bloomer

Age	Total Invested	Amount Available
20	$0	$0
25	$0	$0
30	$2,400	$2,520
35	$14,400	$19,144
40	$26,400	$45,174
45	$38,400	$85,992
50	$50,400	$149,724
55	$62,400	$249,618
60	$74,400	$406,020
65	**$85,000**	**$597,215**

Rate of return is 9% annually.

You might be surprised that the person who only saved for 10 years ended up with significantly more than the person who saved for 35 years but started late. Unfortunately, the majority of Americans do not start saving for their retirement until after their twenties. According to Morning Consult, 61 percent of adults didn't start saving for retirement until their thirties or later.[1] This inability to start saving for the future early leads to a higher savings percentage required later in life. As I have shared earlier, wasting time can be more expensive than wasting money.

Enjoying Life Along the Way

As you continue your consistent walk toward wealth building, we should talk about how you should reenergize and stay motivated throughout my nine-step system.

I am blessed that my wife and I come from similar backgrounds. We were both raised in loving homes and money was not wasted. At the beginning of our marriage, I had one of those nerdy conversations that was far from romantic but has set us up for a life beyond our greatest dreams.

> If we can focus on prioritizing saving and investing in our twenties and thirties, we can let off the savings accelerator in our forties. Do this journey in this disciplined way, and I promise we will travel, spend, and enjoy what we have built.

That simple but powerful conversation changed our life. We spent our twenties and thirties doing exactly what I have created in the FOO. The fun part of life is that if you do this right, you can change those future conversations into the more fun and romantic discussions that keep a marriage exciting and healthy.

In our new phase of marriage, we have date nights and evening discussions centered around updating our travel bucket list or upcoming five-year goals. That may sound boring and weird, but not when we're planning vacations to Europe, Bora Bora, and an Alaskan cruise because our oldest daughter requested it. We now spend more on travel per year than I made in salary out of college. That does not happen without a healthy Army of Dollars driving the financial decision-making.

This leads to a discussion about how you are going to enjoy life while still saving and investing for the future. Saving and investing does not mean that you have to lock yourself inside the four walls of your residence and wait for the timer to strike 15 to 20 years of sacrificial living before you enjoy each stage of life. There is a better way that allows you to live the best life, but one that is also grounded with focus and purpose.

Bedazzle Your Basic Life

There is a line between living a miserly life (think Ebenezer Scrooge) and a bedazzled basic life. I do not want you living such a disciplined financial life that you are not having any fun in those 15 to 20 years. Life moves too fast to not have fun—enjoy each stage of the journey! Plus, living a miserly life would not be healthy or sustainable in the long term. I want you to build a financial life that still has enough margin that you can build memories.

In 2002, my wife and I enjoyed a 10-day tour of Italy. It was absolutely incredible; we started the trip in Venice, then traveled to Florence, Pisa, and closed out in Rome. We did it on the cheap, but still made sure we did all of the must-have experiences:

- Gondola ride
- Saint Mark's Square
- Saint Mark's Basilica
- Michelangelo's David
- Leaning Tower of Pisa
- Colosseum
- Vatican City

And so much more; each day was filled with rich experiences.

We did not stay in the nicest of hotels, we dragged our luggage with us on the cobblestone streets, we haggled and learned to negotiate for tour prices, and we also felt that we got ripped off in some small way in every city we visited. At the time, some of those details were stressful, laughable, and far from feeling luxurious. This may not sound like the perfect vacation, but it is hard to put into words how absolutely incredible that trip was. Here is a secret that you might not have realized that will pay dividends for the rest of your life: Memories blossom! Over time our memories actually become better. They become more sentimental and what we remember is more and more positive. The negative experiences tend to drop off or even become part of the colorful details that make the experience fulfilling.

Yes, some of the details of our trip were stressful, but now those are funny anecdotes I share when I tell a story about our visit to Italy. Remember this the next time you are struggling through the family beach vacation and it is stressful working around the small accommodations or the choice to lug your chairs, coolers, and umbrella to the beach. The messy middle season will pass and the stress and negative thoughts will blossom into warm memories of how sweet and fast moving that phase of life was.

Here is another key observation. I have told Italian travel stories and discussed the trip with wealthy friends who have also been to Italy. Their stories sound very similar to mine except we did it for 70 percent cheaper. My key takeaway is to make sure you take time and resources to build and enjoy each phase of your life. Spend money on travel and hobbies that create memories, but do it in a bedazzled, basic, affordable way that still allows you to save for the future.

Does "88x Over" Only Work for 20-Year-Olds?

Throughout my examples, I have shared how powerful it is to start investing early and often. We even use the teaching illustration that every dollar that a 20-year-old saves for retirement has the potential to become $88 by the time they retire at 65. (We reviewed the concept in Step 2: Max-Out Your Employer Match.)

However, I know that most do not really start investing on their 20th birthday. Does that mean that the opportunity to grow one dollar into $88 over 45 years is lost on the majority of savers and investors? Not necessarily. There is a good chance you started saving something for the future by the time you turned 30. If that is the case, then you can rest assured that a portion of your money will have the required 45 years of growth to reach the 88 times multiple since the average American life expectancy is greater than 75.

- The powerful resource of time does not have to be left only to the young. We know that it typically takes 28 years to make your first million, and the average age to reach seven figures is 49 (according to research and surveys from Ramsey Solutions). Using this 28-year window, millionaire status is accessible to people at many ages. A 35-year-old starting from zero dollars has the potential to reach millionaire status by 63.
- A 40-year-old starting from zero dollars has the potential to reach millionaire status by 68.
- A 45-year-old starting from zero dollars has the potential to reach millionaire status by 73.

This should give you the clarity to start your new and improved wealth-building journey. The absolute best time to invest was yesterday, so that means that the second-best time to invest is today. There will be more opportunities coming if you will allow your money to start doing the heavy lifting of building your Army of Dollars.

Emergency Catch-Up Plan for Those in Their Forties and Fifties

I want everyone to graduate beyond the basics, and I understand that with so much emphasis on time and the value of starting early that anyone picking up this book later in life will feel frustrated. I challenge you to harness the energy of those emotions and create a take-no-prisoners plan to overcome and persevere. Below I have gone beyond warm words of encouragement and created an outline of what actions you can take. This will allow you to avoid missing another day and to take control of your future as quickly as possible.

Determine if You Are Behind, On, or Ahead of the Curve (Know Your Number)

To know where you are going, you first need to determine where you are on the journey to financial independence. There are many variables that go into determining where you are—goals and expectations, current savings/investments, how much you can save going forward, how the investments will perform, and any potential chaos that life could throw at you financially. These components and complications are beyond what I can share in a chapter closing, but fortunately we have a tool and course that will fast-track this process. Check out our Know Your Number tool and course at Learn.MoneyGuy.com. This tool can be the decision center and testing ground for all of the elements of this plan.

Determine What Levers You Control

The Know Your Number tool should give you a good idea of what you can expect with your current assets, savings habits, and changing times (rates of return and inflation). It will also help you know what extending your retirement date or increasing your contributions will do. Both of these components are levers or elements that you control. A valuable exercise is taking complex situations and breaking out the simple controllable elements and solution behaviors. For most financial shortfalls the solutions are simple.

Catch-Up Levers

- Make more money. Increasing your cash flow can allow you to accelerate your savings and investments and catch up to your goals.
- Cut expenses. Decreasing what you spend can also allow you to dedicate more money to accelerate your savings and investments, once again helping you catch up to your desired financial goal.

Modify Your Goal Levers

- Delay your goal. Will extending out your financial independence date by a few years do the trick to provide more time for assets to grow and reach your desired boiling point?
- Lower your future need. You can modify how much you need for independence significantly by squeezing and reducing the annual need from your assets. There are several ways to accomplish and model this:
  - Lower expected future retirement expenses. Maybe you move to a part of the country with a lower cost of living or dramatically reduce retirement expenses by dropping vehicles or other costly expenses.
  - Part-time work or side income. Who says that retirement has to be a full stop on all types of work? If you can keep income flowing, it can directly offset living expenses that would need to be covered by your retirement investments.

› Outside money. There are outside solutions that can help take some of the pressure off your independence goals, such as Social Security and pensions. According to the Center on Budget and Policy Priorities, Social Security benefits replace about 37 percent of past earnings in retirement for those at average earnings. I know that most employers have moved away from defined benefits, but there are quite a few employees that worked for large employers or the government to qualify for some form of retirement benefit.

Army of Dollars

Make your money work as hard as you do. If you are ever going to be able to own your time and live your life on your terms, you need a plan that allows you to step away from the money you make by selling your time, back, and brain for wages and income. The best solution is an Army of Dollars that is working at all hours and days even if you are away. That sounds so simple but, as you have learned, it requires discipline and a commitment to build up this army. Without excuses and distractions, let's make an actionable investment plan.

- Start today. I don't care if it is $50/month, you need to immediately set up a monthly automatic savings and investment plan. If you can save and invest more than that, then do it! The monthly goal needs to be challenging enough that you feel the squeeze of the commitment. I am hopeful that after a few months of success and the ability to see your contributions grow, you will continue to push and increase the monthly investments. If it does not hurt, you are doing it wrong. This new habit is going to be the foundation of your future success. Don't skip leg day—just do it!

- Keep the investments simple. Go back to the beginning of the book where I share the benefits of index investing and then combining that with the easy setup of target retirement funds (index target retirement funds). These investments only require you to share when you need the money (retirement/financial independence) and how much you are investing. They do all of the heavy lifting of asset allocation and updating the investment plan as you approach your goal and your risk profile changes. The biggest low-cost providers of index target retirement funds are Fidelity Investments, Vanguard, and Charles Schwab. That is not an endorsement, but these are good first stops on your research and due-diligence search.
- Ride or die. You are committed to this investment plan, and it does not matter what is going on in the world politically or economically—you will Always Be Buying (ABB, baby!). This plan needs to be emotion proof. I don't care if you are scared or feeling uneasy about what is going on in the world. You will be rewarded by staying committed and loyal to this energized goal to catch up and finally create a plan that will take you beyond dreaming of financial independence.

PART 2

Beyond the Basics

CHAPTER 8

Step 6: Max-Out Retirement Options

> 7 in 10 pre-retirees say they aren't well prepared for their retirement.
>
> 1 in 7 U.S. retirees (ages 65+) live in poverty.
>
> **—LIMRA's Secure Retirement Institute**[1]

Step 6 Preview and What to Know:

No pain, no gain! Building assets for financial independence is a big goal requiring a plan to maximize all of the tax benefits and growth opportunities. This step will explore other retirement plans and strategies to build more tax-advantaged dollars. I also share a net worth template to track your wealth-building journey. Now that you have graduated beyond the basics, your net worth will be your dashboard to know where you are financially. Are you saving enough? Are your investment accounts growing fast enough for retirement? Are debts being paid down fast enough for retirement goals? This chapter will maximize the tools of retirement so you can know where you are and stay on the accelerated path.

There is a crisis in America. Our friends, neighbors, and co-workers are not saving for retirement. My goal is to help you understand wealth creation, the discipline and deferred gratification required, and assist you in unleashing the power of your Army of Dollars. It only requires saving a little bit of today for a more beautiful tomorrow!

Ramsey Solutions shares in *Everyday Millionaires* that eight out of 10 millionaires reached that status by investing in their employer-sponsored retirement plans. It is also interesting that the average age of crossing into seven-figure millionaire status is 49.[2] I have mentioned these data points multiple times because they cut through the noise of our social media world and instant gratification. These two stats confirm that wealth creation and financial independence are typically built in the long term. There are not any get-rich-quick schemes that show up in any of our research. The core components of discipline, money, and time are your ingredients to create financial independence.

Track Your Net Worth

Does your money work as hard as you do? Tracking your net worth every year is a success habit that will be one of your biggest wealth-building tools. To help you get started, we've included a net worth template in the appendix. You can also download a free copy at MoneyGuy.com/MillionaireDownloads. For a more advanced net worth tool that helps with tracking and even provides feedback on your progress, consider checking out our Net Worth Tool at Learn.MoneyGuy.com. First, tracking your net worth gives you a dashboard view of annual changes and how your financial health is progressing. Are there areas that should be growing faster? I also love to review the change in account value from the accounts appreciating and growing. Do this long enough and there will be a few key milestones. You will remember the first time that your account appreciates more than what you make in a week from working. Consider what this means—instead of you working with your back, brain, or hands, you made money through your Army of Dollars. That week's worth of work will then turn into a month of wages, and you will quickly know you are approaching financial independence when your Army of Dollars from your investments is growing annually more than what you make in a year of working.

There are a ton of analogies and similarities between exercising to build muscle and good financial habits to build wealth. However, there is a crucial difference from the starting line. When you start exercising, it will take months to see the dramatic physical changes. This delayed gratification often leads to a drop-off in your discipline and commitment. On the other hand, you will immediately notice benefits if you prepare a net worth statement, build a budget, and turn these behaviors into consistent financial habits. You will not waste as much money on frivolous purchases, you will feel the nudge to invest more with the new cash flow savings, and you will love seeing the debt melt away. It will be exciting in the short term and rewarding over the long term with exponential wealth-building benefits. I share these tools and behaviors that create success to encourage you not to make the mistakes of your peers. Most are not thinking about creating financial independence and the opportunity of retirement until the easy opportunity has passed. If you follow my nudge to improve your discipline and use the tools to create traction, your small changes today will create exponential long-term growth.

Maxing-Out Retirement Means Inevitable Wealth

It is important to remember that our tax code heavily incentivizes you to save for the future and for your employer to prime the pump of your success by participating in your retirement savings and even encouraging your participation. In Step 2 we maximized the free money component, but there are still more benefits we need to explore.

I mentioned that the first account in which most millionaires cross seven-figure status is their employer retirement plan. Yes, the free money from your employer is an effective fire starter, but the feature that fuels and stokes the wealth-building blaze most is the fact that these accounts encourage repeated positive habits over and over again, and they make the process easy. Success loves a good "set it and forget it" strategy. You "set it" by setting up an automatic paycheck deduction. The "forget it" part of employer-sponsored plans is especially effective given that access is age restricted (usually around 55 to 59.5) and the money is automatically invested, completing the Always Be Buying process that leverages time and compounding growth. Combining these ingredients is the recipe for creating inevitable millionaire wealth.

Limiting Bad Habits with Forced Scarcity

Have you ever limited what food makes it into your kitchen so you can stick to your healthier eating plan? Perhaps you cut out the sweet cereals and snacks like chips that are impossible to stop at one or fifty, or you completely avoided the ice cream aisle of your grocery store. All of these behaviors are creating a plan of scarcity—a plan to keep you away from your bad habits and foods that will derail your healthy new lifestyle. We can tap into this same discipline with our money and create a system that restricts access to resources so they are not wasted on bad financial habits.

The powerful behavioral component of retirement plans is how they encourage good habits and keep them rolling no matter what is going on in your life. Along with creating easy-to-follow, positive habits, your retirement plan can set up a counter system that limits and even restricts bad habits. After all, as humans, it is so much easier for us to focus on the satisfaction and enjoyment from instant gratification, even if it is to the detriment of our long-term financial success. You can immediately experience the joy of not saving and, instead, eating out or buying a new outfit. Meanwhile, increasing your retirement contributions is going to take years to see the benefit. Even though the long-term benefit is exponentially bigger and better than the instant gratification, we need a way to offset the logic disconnect or lack of discipline of our behavior. It is time to introduce you to my habit-building secret weapon: Forced Scarcity!

Forced Scarcity is the process of creating and expanding your automatic saving and investment plans as your income increases. This simple but very effective tool allows you to cut lifestyle creep off at the knees. You are increasing the good and healthy wealth-building habits by consistently adding to investments as your income increases while at the same time limiting your access to free cash flow that can be spent on bad and unnecessary wants and behaviors.

The next time you get a pay raise, give the 60/40 rule a try. Allocate 60 percent of the income increase toward increasing your retirement plan contributions (add a few percentage points to your retirement contribution rate). This simple exercise is a win-win since you are allowing yourself to enjoy an improved lifestyle with the 40 percent increase, but the lion's share is being used to maximize your journey to financial independence.

Forced Scarcity is effective outside of retirement accounts, too. I introduced this powerful behavioral tool here because it is easy to set up within your employer retirement plan. However, as you start stacking success and even progress to Step 7 (Hyper-Accumulation), you will find that this works as you start building your other accounts, including your taxable brokerage account.

At our firm, we help employers set up retirement plans and often talk to the participants of those plans. I'm always amazed when they share that once the savings habit is started, they barely notice the missing money; and then one day, they are shocked at how big their retirement assets have become.

Every year, there is a maximum elective deferral you can contribute to your employer-provided retirement plan. For example, if you were under 50 in 2024, you could contribute up to $23,000 to your 401(k) or 403(b)—that comes out to $1,916.67 per month.

If you are 50 and over, you get access to an annual catch-up contribution. As the name implies, the government recognizes you are approaching retirement and saving has likely become more of a priority. As a result, the government allows you the opportunity to save more than what younger workers can save. In 2024, that catch-up contribution is $7,500 (or simply $625 more per month), for a total annual contribution from salary deferrals (your contributions) of $30,500.

Employer-Provided Roth Retirement Plans

These are qualified accounts, including 401(k), 403(b), or governmental 457(b) plans, that hold designated Roth contributions. When you set up your employer-provided retirement account, you will be given the choice for your contributions to be deposited as traditional pre-tax (take a tax deduction now, but pay higher ordinary income taxes on future withdrawals) or Roth (no tax deduction when contributions are made but tax-free growth withdrawals in the future). In 2024, the funding limit for qualified Roth contributions is $23,000 plus an additional $7,500 catch-up contribution if you are 50 or over. These amounts will also be adjusted up in future years to account for changes in cost of living and inflation.

What makes qualified Roth accounts super exciting for higher-income savers is that there are no income limits. You can make any sum of money and still contribute to these plans. You can also contribute to and max-out contributions to both your Roth IRA and the Roth portion of your employer plan in the same year as long as you are mindful of the Roth IRA income limits discussed earlier.

How Do You Choose Between a Roth or Traditional Option?

Deciding between Roth and traditional options depends on your specific financial situation, goals, and tax outlook. However, I can share some general guidance for you to consider and then customize for your personal long-term goals. Below I have compiled a few of the key factors to consider when making this important decision.

Consider Marginal Tax Rates

Ask yourself the following questions about your tax rates:

- What is your federal marginal tax rate (tax rate you pay on the next dollar of income)?
- What is your state marginal tax rate (also the tax rate you pay on the next dollar of income)?
- What is your tax outlook, or how do you expect your taxes to change in the future?

Why do these factors matter? You will want to add your two marginal tax rates together. If your combined (federal and state) marginal tax rate is greater than 30 percent, you are in what is considered a higher tax bracket. The higher your tax bracket, the more beneficial the current-year tax deduction is from traditional (non-Roth) contributions. The tax outlook comes into play because we are currently in a historical low-tax-rate environment.

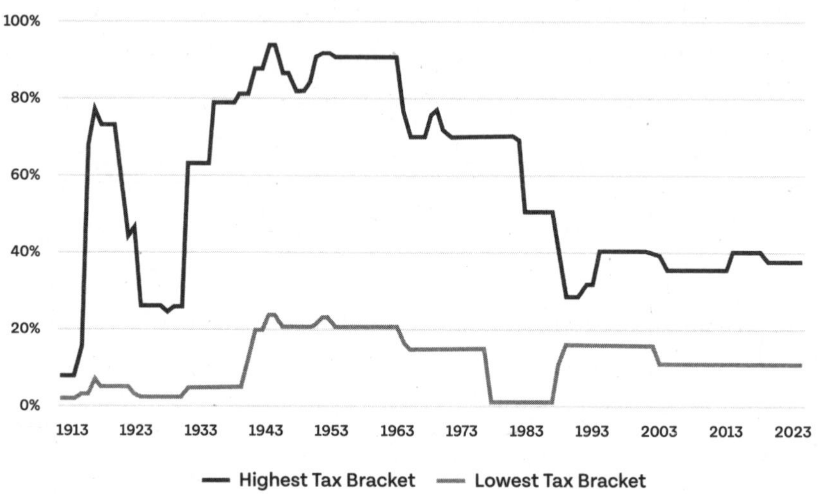

Get Nerdy and Understand 415 Limits

IRC (Internal Revenue Code) Section 415 limits are always a great conversation drop-in at parties and social gatherings. No matter what the topic of discussion, mentioning 415 limits will make you seem smarter. In all seriousness, these limits are important, especially in this new world that we live in where most people have side hustles and multiple employers. Here is what the IRS shares about this key limit:

> Total annual additions to a participant's defined contribution plan account are limited to the dollar amount imposed by IRC Section 415(c).

What this means is that every year there is a limit to what you can contribute to your employer-provided retirement plans. Your personal contributions (salary deferrals) are capped at the annual limit (in 2024, that number is $23,000, or $30,500 for those 50 and over) no matter how many employers or sources of income you have. In other words, you are limited to $23,000 in contributions even if you have multiple sources of income. For example, if you have a day job that offers a 401(k) and you max it out, you would not be allowed to make contributions to another 401(k) or 403(b) plan in the same year, even if it were from a different employer or a different job.

There is a key element of 415 limits that can be taken advantage of by side hustlers and gig economy workers, though. You may not be able to make personal contributions through additional salary deferrals, but you could make additional contributions on the employer-funded side.

When you work for yourself through a side hustle, you are likely treated as an independent contractor and paid through a 1099-MISC or 1099-NEC. Working as an independent contractor has downsides: you are not provided any employee benefits (retirement, vacation, and healthcare) and you are responsible for paying both the employer and employee portion of Social Security and Medicare taxes. Due to this completely independent structure, you are viewed as both the employee and the employer of your small business. This arrangement provides a few key planning opportunities. As the employer, you are allowed to set up a retirement plan that will legally help you offset tax obligations and save more for retirement. If you are an independent contractor or have other eligible self-employment income, there are two key account structures you should become familiar with:

- **SEP-IRA/SEPs (Simplified Employee Pension Plans).** These allow you to essentially go back in time for tax savings. If you are working on your income taxes for the previous year and realize your income was higher than anticipated due to 1099 work, you have the ability to open and contribute to a SEP-IRA to lower last year's taxes. SEPs do not have 415 limit issues since all contributions are from employers only (no employee contributions allowed).

SEP-IRA contributions only come in the deductible pre-tax structure. There are not any tax-free Roth contributions allowed. They also count as IRA accounts, so they can prevent you from implementing a Roth IRA conversion strategy (also known as a backdoor Roth contribution) for higher-income families that seek to fund tax-free Roth accounts annually.

- **Solo 401(k).** These allow salary-deferral contributions, but if you maxed-out those contributions with your primary employer, this will not be utilized. You will likely only be using the employer-funding portion or after-tax contributions if you are seeking to implement the mega backdoor Roth funding strategy. This unique planning opportunity allows you to convert massive amounts of after-tax qualified contributions into tax-free Roth assets. However, it is not a simple process and has limitations—search our content at MoneyGuy.com to find more details and planning specifics.

  Even though Solo 401(k) employer-funded contributions are traditionally pre-tax, they do not count as IRA assets. This means the Roth conversion strategy (also known as a backdoor Roth contribution) is not impacted.

  Solo 401(k)s cannot have employees other than owners and spouses.

  Solo 401(k)s are exempt from the complicated testing and annual tax filing as long as the accounts are less than $250,000. Once these accounts exceed that level, you will want to make sure you keep up with annual filing requirements since the penalties are severe.

Unveiling the Power of the 457 Double-Savings Hack

There is a way to fund two retirement plans with employee salary deferral contributions in a single year. We described earlier that you are not allowed to load up two 401(k)s or 403(b)s in a single year and exceed the contribution limit ($23,000 in 2024). The way around that? Fund a retirement plan that is set up under a completely different part of the tax code.

Enter 457 plans. These are retirement plans available for state and local governments and tax-exempt nongovernmental entities. I have seen quite a few government, hospitals, universities, and other public service employers that offer employees access to both 401(k)s or 403(b)s and 457 plans. Why is this such a big deal for higher-income employees? These structures allow employees to fully fund both accounts with salary deferrals, which means $23,000 to their 401(k), and then contributions up to $23,000 into the 457 plan in the same year. This double funding is a unique savings opportunity. It does require a larger income to have the margin to be able to max-out two retirement plans in a year; however, we see clients every year that have both the access and the income to take advantage of this tremendous savings hack. It is also useful to know that 457 plans do not have the same early withdrawal restrictions of ages 55 and 59.5 that other retirement accounts have.

What Does Maxing-Out Look Like

The illustration on the next page is a great way to see what maxing-out your 401(k) has the potential to become. Let's assume two spouses decide to max-out their 401(k) accounts. They both contribute the 2023 limit of $22,500, or $45,000 total between the two. All contributions earn an 8 percent annual rate of return over the long term. What does that have the opportunity to become?!

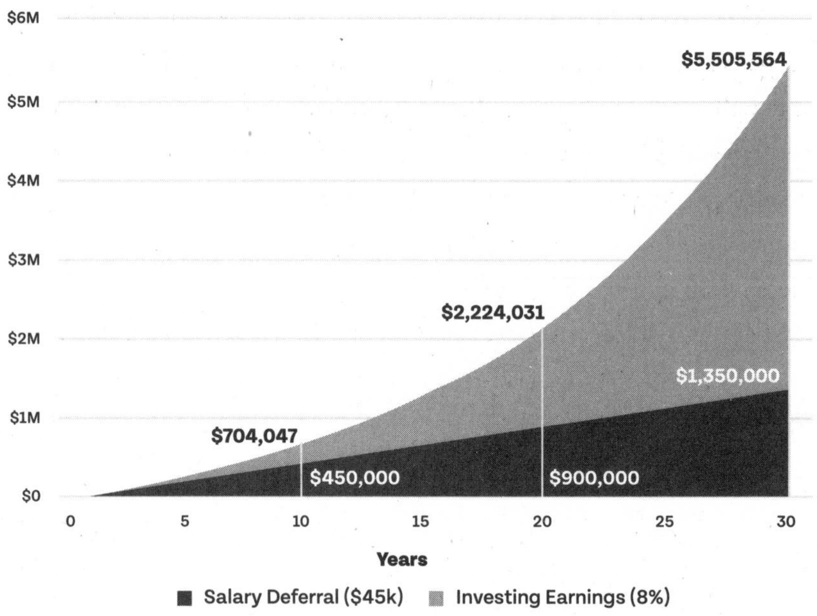

Over 30 years, they contributed $1,350,000 to their 401(k) accounts. After 30 years of contributions and growth of 8 percent annually, their 401(k) accounts are worth over $5,500,000! Maybe now you understand why so many millionaires first reach that milestone within their 401(k)s.

How Do You Graduate to the Next Step of the FOO?

In this chapter, we have laid out lofty goals of maxing-out your retirement accounts. It is easy to say, "Make sure you fully fund your 401(k) and contribute the maximum $23,000 in 2024." However, if you are an overachiever in your savings goals, but your income is less than six figures, this can feel like an unrealistic request. To close out, I want to clarify the concept of maximizing your retirement options and how to know when you have graduated to Leveraging Hyper-Accumulation, the next step in the FOO.

The goal of Step 6 is to ensure that you are saving and investing 25 percent for retirement and financial independence. There is a chance you will graduate beyond this step with minimal additional work if you have already done the hard work of building healthy savings and investment habits in earlier steps of the FOO. Imagine you are fresh out of school and your annual salary is $40,000. You have already completed Step 2 of the FOO by contributing 6 percent of your pay to your employer-provided retirement plan in order to maximize the fifty cents of every dollar match up to 6 percent of your pay. You also completed Step 5 by contributing $7,000 to your Roth IRA. As a percentage of your income, you are saving more than 25 percent ($10,600) of your $40,000 gross income: $2,400 401(k) savings + $1,200 employer match + $7,000 Roth IRA contribution.

This 25 percent annual, automatic funding percentage exceeds our suggested 20–25 percent of gross income to successfully fund your Army of Dollars for long-term success.

The Larger the Income, the Bigger the Responsibility

Another influence on savings rates is how much income you create annually. The higher your income, the further you are from the government's safety net benefits (Social Security), and more of your financial responsibility rests on your shoulders. Once you make over $100,000 per individual or $200,000 as a household, you should no longer count employer contributions in your annual savings percentage calculation (unless you are the employer and controlling how the funding occurs, and it is well beyond 25 percent of gross income). The higher your income, the more you should shoot for maxing-out all retirement contributions. This includes IRAs, Health Savings Accounts (HSAs), and employer retirement plans.

Much of the FOO and the Financial Mutant mindset are designed for those who do not struggle with basic behavioral discipline and have no problem sacrificing a small portion of today for a better future. This core behavior and understanding will help you power through the struggles that will occur later with increased success. If you can build good financial habits while you are young and broke, the side effects and complexities of success are minimized in the future.

Use the checklist that follows as you think about contributing more to your employer plan and potentially maxing it out and beyond.

Maximizing Employer-Sponsored Accounts

☐ **Know your combined marginal tax rate.**

Add together your top marginal state, federal, and local income tax rates. If this number is above 30%, consider contributing to the pretax portion of your plan. If it is under 25%, consider the Roth portion. If you are in between, consider other factors, like your current account structure and retirement goals.

☐ **Max-out your plan—but be careful.**

Once you know which "bucket" of your employer plan you will be contributing to, you can start working toward maximizing your account. Be careful, though: with some plans, you could lose out on employer matching funds by maxing-out too early in the year.

☐ **Contribute more at age 50.**

Once you reach the year you will turn 50, you can make extra catch-up contributions. If you are already maxing-out your plan, try to take full advantage of these extra catch-up contributions.

☐ **Consider the mega backdoor Roth strategy.**
After reaching your maximum annual salary deferrals, you may be able to build even more tax-advantaged retirement dollars with what's known as the mega backdoor Roth strategy. Check with your employer to see if they allow after-tax contributions and in-service distributions. As I shared earlier, this unique planning opportunity allows you to convert massive amounts of after-tax qualified contributions into tax-free Roth assets. However, it is not a simple process and has limitations—search our content at MoneyGuy.com to find more details and planning specifics.

Focus on the habit of saving and saving inside of retirement accounts so that you can reach that 20–25 percent of gross income threshold as soon as possible. Once you accomplish this goal, you will graduate to FOO Step 7: Leverage Hyper-Accumulation.

CHAPTER 9

Step 7: Building That More Beautiful Tomorrow (Leverage Hyper-Accumulation)

> Today I will do what others won't, so tomorrow I will do what others can't.
>
> **—Jerry Rice**

Step 7 Preview and What to Know:

Success creates complications! Fortunately, this step will guide you through what to do once you're saving greater than 25 percent of your income. Learn about each of the three savings buckets and how to leverage each to maximize the legal limits of tax savings now and in retirement. I also share four hacks, which are the keys to unlocking financial happiness. This chapter will challenge you to map out the what and the "why" of your goals, to differentiate between happiness and fulfillment, and to trade your money for time and freedom.

Congratulations, You Are Rich!

If you have made it to Step 7—Hyper-Accumulation—this means you are now saving more than 25 percent of your gross income. With Hyper-Accumulation, you have an income that allows you to cover your living expenses, and you have enough margin to save for the future. Now that you can invest at this advanced level, your money can work even harder for you. Step 7 is the first step of walking into abundance.

When we see folks driving around in nice luxury cars or living in large homes, we are given the impression that they are "rich." But "rich" really just means that you have the income to cover the expenses of your life. If you can afford to drive a Porsche and live in a 7,000-square-foot house, you have all of the outward trappings of being rich. This tendency to flex or show how successful you are has been baked into our culture as a result of the consumer society we live in. However, being rich doesn't necessarily mean you are wealthy. If you are required to work to make money to cover your monthly debt payments on your fancy "rich" life, I would argue that you are missing the point and difference between looking rich and having wealth. Wealth is the component of money that has significantly more mystery to it. Wealth is the unseen resource (Army of Dollars) hidden away from the public's view that allows you *to live life on your terms*. As we will learn, living life on your terms is more valuable than flashy, expensive objects and is often overlooked. The vast majority of Americans trade their time and labor for money for basic survival. It is a transaction made out of obligation in order to pay their bills and keep food on the table. This setup means you do not truly own your life or how you get to allocate your time and labor. You are a servant to your financial obligations. Building true wealth puts you on the other side of the equation. If you can save and build enough investments that earn more than your labor and more than what you need to pay your bills, you are at financial independence. Now you can trade your money for time and freedom. You are not obligated to work anymore. If you choose to work, it is for the joy and satisfaction you get from the activity. This is what we are aspiring to build—the true abundance of owning your time and living your best life on your terms. Time is an invaluable, limited resource, and the ability to trade money for time is extremely powerful. Don't let society or the expectation of what "rich" looks like dictate your financial decision-making. Break the mold and embrace your inner Financial Mutant.

The Need for Hyper-Accumulation

With the scarcity of pensions and long-term uncertainty of Social Security, the majority of us will have to build and provide our own assets for financial independence. You should aspire to reach hyper-saver status by saving 25 percent of your gross annual income. Retirement assets such as 401(k)s, 403(b)s, and Roth IRAs will provide the foundation for those savings goals. Their tax benefits and consistent monthly Always Be Buying contributions make them extremely powerful. However, even retirement accounts have limitations. You may find that you have maxed-out all allowed annual contributions, or you realize that all of your assets are in restricted retirement accounts. It would be nice to have assets with more flexibility, including no contribution limits, no age restrictions, and no penalty for early withdrawal. Fortunately, the taxable brokerage account checks the boxes on all of these needs.

The taxable brokerage account is the future flexibility tool that is often underutilized and not fully appreciated. It offers the following benefits:

- No limits on account contributions
- Limited compliance or maintenance cost—just make sure you report the income on your annual tax return

- Opens up additional planning tools, including tax-loss harvesting (more on this coming) and donating appreciated assets to your favorite charities
- Still tax favored with lower tax rates on dividends and capital gains
- No holding periods or age restrictions to keep you from accessing your money early

At a certain point, you will likely adjust your monthly savings plans to include opening an individual or joint investment account to complete your accumulation goals and fill in this pre-age-55 gap.

Unlocking Financial Flexibility: Embracing the Power of Liquidity

We love building savings in a taxable brokerage account because it also creates more flexibility for liquidity and offers easier access to capital than retirement accounts if you are under 59.5. It is not uncommon for long-term savers to realize in their thirties and forties that the lion's share of their assets are in restricted tax-deferred employer plans or retirement accounts (Roth IRAs). Who can blame you? The long-term growth and tax benefits are too powerful to ignore. From time to time, we'll get new clients with seven-figure retirement accounts, but no access to cash or investments for the kids' education or even buying another vehicle. If all you have are retirement accounts, then every dollar you need to access early becomes very expensive because of taxes and penalties. This can become a major problem if you plan on retiring early, but savings in a taxable brokerage account can create the bridge that allows you access to your investments earlier than the normal ages 55 and 59.5 provided in your qualified retirement accounts.

The Different Savings Buckets

Diversification in account types is very important to understand. Here are your three main buckets:

Three Taxable Buckets

The three ways to build wealth.

Tax-Deferred Account   Taxable Account   Tax-Free Account

Tax-Deferred Accounts

Tax-deferred accounts include traditional 401(k)s, 403(b)s, IRAs, and rollover IRAs. These accounts grow without taxes on annual income or appreciation, and the tax deductions for contributions are powerful. There are, however, multiple holes in this savings bucket that you need to consider.

- You'll pay income tax on any withdrawals when you pull that money out of the account.
- Required Minimum Distributions (RMDs) begin at age 72–75, depending on when you were born, to force your hand on taking withdrawals and paying taxes.
- When you pass away and your heirs inherit this account, they also inherit the RMDs and will have to pay income taxes on the distributions.

Tax-Free Accounts

Tax-free accounts include employer-provided Roth plans, Roth IRAs, and HSAs. These accounts do not receive any tax deductions in the year of contributions (Roth accounts), or they have to be used for healthcare (HSAs), but they grow completely tax free. The government severely restricts who can fund these accounts and how much they can contribute.

Taxable Brokerage Account

Taxable brokerage accounts include individual and joint investment accounts as well as trust accounts. If you're in a lower tax bracket, there's an opportunity for lower investment tax rates on dividends and capital gains. If structured properly, there is even an opportunity for a zero percent capital gains tax rate if your taxable income is low enough to qualify. These accounts are very flexible in providing access to liquidity. They do have a tax headwind: all income (dividends, interest, and capital gains from trades) is taxed in the current year.

Which Assets to Place in Each Bucket

This step of the Financial Order of Operations (FOO) is also the point in your financial life that asset location will become even more important. Different asset types behave differently from a tax perspective, so placing them inside the right bucket can serve to optimize your lifetime wealth-building potential. If you can save in all three buckets, you can create a tremendous long-term planning opportunity. There is a chance that you will be able to manipulate the tax code legally by strategically pulling out of different accounts in retirement. This will allow you to maximize your Roth conversion opportunities or maximize the zero percent capital gains rate on your taxable brokerage accounts, too.

Tax-deferred accounts are a great place to keep conservative, fixed-income holdings. These assets generate income that is taxed at ordinary income tax rates, so the tax-deferred accounts are ideal holding accounts from a tax perspective given they are also taxed at ordinary income tax rates.

We all want to maximize tax-free growth, as tax-free accounts are awesome wealth-building tools. Load up these accounts with your long-term growth assets. Be careful of speculation because you are unable to take losses from a Roth account. Balance the desire to see assets exponentially grow tax-free through compounding growth without going so far out on the risk spectrum that you buy risky speculative investments that are just as likely to be worthless as they are to explode in value.

In taxable accounts, you'll keep cash reserves needed for any upcoming major expenses. This is also the best account structure to hold dividend-paying assets and appreciating assets that will be subject to lower long-term capital gains rates.

Graduating Past Index Target Retirement Funds

As you likely noticed, success does have an unfortunate side effect: additional complexity. As we close out Step 7, Hyper-Accumulation, it is important to let you know you are likely approaching an important graduation point and milestone in your long-term journey of building and growing wealth.

You have reached the point of sophistication where it makes sense to go beyond index target retirement funds. This is also the point where your financial enterprise has reached a certain level of complexity and you may want to consider bringing in the help of a financial professional. The following are a few indicators of when you have reached the point of graduation:

- Account structure and tax location matters in your upcoming retirement plan.
- If you are part of the Financial Independence Retire Early (FIRE) movement, you will need an asset structure plan that allows access to assets before the age of 59.5 so you can make withdrawals without penalty.
- You want to lower your annual tax bill by structuring your asset allocation in coordination with your different asset location options (as we just reviewed).
- Tax-loss harvesting has become more important to how you manage your investment holdings. Tax-loss harvesting is a technique that savvy investors use to offset their capital gains and reduce their overall taxable income. When you sell an investment at a loss, you can use that loss to offset any capital gains you may have realized throughout the year. If your losses exceed your gains, you can use them to offset up to $3,000 of your regular income, effectively lowering your taxable income. Why would you want to intentionally sell investments at a loss? This is especially valuable during volatile investment periods. It allows you to sell the down holdings and buy into other investments to catch the market recovery, and it allows you to turn that lemon into some lemonade for your tax situation.
- You would like to create a charitable giving plan that includes donating appreciated holdings from your taxable accounts.

Understanding the Pitfalls of Lottery Dreams

How often have you daydreamed about what it would be like to be rich? Growing up, I watched Robin Leach and *Lifestyles of the Rich and Famous* and then along came MTV's *Cribs*. It was fascinating to see all the beautiful homes, exotic cars, and over-the-top lifestyles (but I discovered later that most of it was staged and fake).

How many of us have participated in the office lotto pool, hoping to fund these caviar dreams? It is fun to daydream about spending money on a lavish life. However, studies have shown that lottery winners typically turn out to be financial failures. According to research from CNBC, "lottery winners are more likely to declare bankruptcy within three to five years than the average American. What's more, studies have shown that winning the lottery does not necessarily make you happier or healthier."[1]

Wow! There is a ton to unpack in those two sentences. First, how do you go broke if someone drops a windfall of money on you? And why are you not happier? Having more money is supposed to be better than less money, right? The answers are simpler than we all realize. Most lottery winners enjoy the concept of spending large sums of money. Said another way, they like looking rich but have no knowledge about how to stay wealthy. They have not matured in their relationship with money to learn the healthy balance of what money can provide over the long term to cover living expenses, and also to know what money can and cannot provide emotionally for happiness and fulfillment.

There is a reason that we have seen this failure repeated by celebrities and sports stars who come into large sums of money. Consumption can feel good in the short term (strong instant gratification), but it doesn't have the staying power of a life well lived with the wisdom learned of what creates financial abundance—abundance that can last beyond your lifetime. Building abundance means having enough to cover your financial needs (knowing what is enough) and then also going much deeper into the emotional components of money and building wealth. What is your "why" and how big a life do you need to be content? Everyone should be self-aware to understand that you can buy yourself out of wealth if your monthly cost to cover the loan payments, maintenance, and ongoing expenses of your stuff exceeds what is sustainable over the long term. Does that mean that living like a miser will fix all of these errors and lead to a life of success, happiness, and fulfillment? Nope! The answer is more nuanced, and we should explore the root of happiness so you can build your abundance plan that reflects both.

There Is a Difference Between Happiness and Fulfillment

It is not surprising to find out that most of us are striving for the wrong goal or using an inappropriate scale for success.

It makes sense; I have navigated my own wealth-building journey and helped families that have all the trappings of success. This experience has cultivated a rare knowledge that most people don't have. First, there is a human need to have the basics covered. The emotional well-being of not being stressed about how you will pay for your next meal or provide shelter for your family gets you to the first milestone of financial happiness. If you spend any time exploring financial content, you have likely seen the debate on the 2010 study by Princeton psychologist Daniel Kahneman claiming that $75,000 was the amount of income at which emotional well-being stopped increasing. Unfortunately, the financial media and social media used the research to declare that this was the threshold for happiness. "Happiness" seems like a strong word for this. "Basics covered" seems more appropriate. Income over $75,000 may not change a person's day-to-day emotional well-being or contentment, but there is an impact on their life satisfaction level (things are moving in the right direction).

Contentment and covering basic necessities still feels a long way from the escapism and excitement that lottery daydreams envision. Big spending and buying cool stuff may seem like a component of runaway success, but it is actually a distraction from the simple component that actually creates what we all desire. The answer lies in whether or not you are living a purposeful life on your terms.

When we all think about the relationship between money, happiness, and purpose, we quickly realize that the milestone most of us crave is fulfillment. We want to feel that we are doing what we were put on this Earth to do and that we control the direction of our lives. Happiness and fulfillment come by living your best life on your terms. Do you get to spend the most valuable resource—time—doing what you want? Your job will be more enjoyable when you are working out of choice, passion, and desire instead of the obligation to pay the bills.

That desire to build the more beautiful tomorrow with a bit of discipline and sacrifice today is why we make the choice to save, invest, and build our Army of Dollars. All of this is so you can understand that wealth creation and asset building is so much more powerful than what others know about your lifestyle or even what they think about you. Here are four financial happiness hacks:

1. **Focus on experiences rather than things.** Why experiences? First, eager anticipation and planning can be just as fun as the trip or experience itself. Second, as I previously shared, the memories you make will actually improve (blossom) over time as minor annoyances fade away and the good memories remain.
2. **Underindulge.** Living on less than you make (deferred gratification) is not only the foundation of wealth building but also of happiness. Riches and wealth are often the side effects of a fulfilling life, not the other way around.
3. **Spend money on others.** It truly is better to give than receive. Spending on others feels good and creates positive physical and mental reactions within your body (almost like we were designed for this).

4. **Faith, family, community, and work.** Thinking of things not of this world, the connections of strong relationships, and waking up with purpose, knowing that how you spend your time at work is making the world better can go a long way toward building contentment and silencing the noise of our consumption-driven society.

Mapping a Path to Living "On Your Terms"

Have you ever sat down and pondered what living "on your terms" actually means for you? Hyper-Accumulation can mean different things for different folks. Do you know what you are working toward or the "why" of your lifestyle and savings decisions? It is hard to navigate a long-term journey without the focus and direction of planning and mapping a path forward. Your homework for this chapter is to think long and hard about what you want to accomplish with your financial resources. The fact that you are in the Hyper-Accumulation step shows you have the tools to reach those goals.

Hyper-Accumulation

- [ ] **Are you investing 25% of your income?**
To be considered a Hyper-Accumulator, you need to be investing at least 25% of your income for retirement. Depending on your income, you may not need to maximize your employer-sponsored account to reach 25%.

- [ ] **Are you investing what you need?**
Depending on your retirement goals, you may need to be saving more than 25%. Use our Know Your Number course, at Learn.MoneyGuy.com, to help inform your savings rate.

☐ **How will pensions and other income factor into your plan?**
If you work for the federal government or an employer that offers a generous pension, Hyper-Accumulation may look different for you than it does for someone without a pension. Know what to expect in retirement and how these promised retirement cash flow sources could be used to offset or reduce the retirement expenses your investment assets will need to cover.

☐ **Do you understand the three taxable buckets?**
At this stage in your financial journey, you need to understand the taxable buckets and what assets are more appropriate in each.

- Tax deferred. This includes pre-tax accounts like pre-tax 401(k)s and pre-tax IRAs. Include assets that generate ordinary income.
- Tax free. Accounts include Roth accounts and HSAs. Consider holding high-flying growth assets here.
- After tax. Taxable brokerage accounts. Include assets with more favorable tax treatment and liquidity.

CHAPTER 10

Step 8: Funding the Abundance Goals (Prepay Future Expenses)

> Someone's sitting in the shade today because someone planted a tree a long time ago.
>
> **—Warren Buffett**

Step 8 Preview and What to Know:

Welcome to the fun stage of abundance! This step encourages you to start dreaming. Perhaps you wish to save for your children or take that big trip you always imagined. How about driving a car that can be considered a splurge? Whatever your future has in store for you, you'll learn how to plan for it and understand what options you have within that journey. Take a look at how your dedication to discipline, money, and time has, and will continue to, benefit you.

Congratulations on graduating to Step 8 of the Financial Order of Operations (FOO): Prepay Future Expenses! Your early sacrifice is now generating financial fruit. Instead of stressing out about how to cover the basics, you are now officially in the fun stage of abundance where it's time to start dreaming. You have margin, and margin gives you options. What do you want to do with your money and time, and what does that mean for the long term? Step 8 is also the chance to help out those we love in a healthy way. It is now time to turn that extra financial margin into a force of positive energy.

Beyond YOLO: Embracing Financial Mutancy for Life on Your Terms

Anyone else get annoyed with YOLO? It is usually thrown out as a way to justify a bad decision, in an interview of a young person doing something extremely dangerous, or on the comment pages of our *Money Guy Show* YouTube channel. On YouTube, we get comments that share they are living for today because "tomorrow is not promised."

I always chuckle to myself because life is quite humbling. Statistically, most of the YOLO crowd will likely live to a ripe old age. Life expectancy in the US has doubled in the last century and a half.[1] Americans are living longer and will spend more time in retirement, not working, than earlier generations. That point of clarity can go one of two ways:

1. If the YOLO crowd hasn't planned well and respected the ingredients of success (discipline, money, and time), they will lean into self-coping tools and limiting beliefs, such as "the world is against them," "the system is rigged," and they "never had a chance." Those who believe this feel that it is never their fault, and typically they are more than willing to share their bitter tale with any young person who cares to listen. Unfortunately, the

majority of our peers are absolutely dreadful with money, and therefore this narrative has worked its way into our social conversation. It doesn't help that wealth is secretive, and it is taboo to discuss money openly.

2. On the happier road less traveled are the Financial Mutants who sacrificed a small portion of their earnings, invested, and patiently waited for wealth to create green shoots. Before they knew it, the earning power of their Army of Dollars was rivaling what they could create with their personal hard work. It is truly glorious, and the accelerating growth will exceed their greatest dreams! A large part of this fulfillment is that they get to do life completely on their terms. And they get to share their successes with others.

The older you get, the more you will start to recognize time as your most precious resource. It powers your financial growth but, unfortunately, it is not replenishable.

If you only live once, don't you want to make sure you spend that time wisely and allocate resources well? That means both maximizing and enjoying each day, but not forgetting the "why" and purpose of each dollar that you built. It means investing in loved ones and experiences, but still making sure to plan ahead to know where you are and where you are going on your abundance journey.

The following are common abundance goals to consider in Step 8.

Time to Help the Kids

It is not uncommon for savers to get distracted from the importance of building their own personal financial foundation because they want to help their children. We have spent the previous seven steps working to make sure you have your retirement squared away first. The savings goal of helping one's kids is pretty far down on our list, and this is surprising to many people.

The moment the kids are born, your world changes. This unconditional love can make financial prioritization hard. However, just like on an airplane, you need to make sure you have on your oxygen mask before you try to help your children or other loved ones. I gave a FOO presentation to a group of engineers, and one asked, "Does this mean we cannot start saving for our kids' college until we are fully funding our Roths, 401(k)s, and savings? That seems cruel to be saving 40 percent of our income for the future and not saving a penny for the kids!" It is completely acceptable to start funding the kids' college tuition and weddings after you are saving 25 percent toward the long term. It is okay to spend a bit more on yourself, too. Remember though, you don't want to forgo your own savings and leave your adult children with the financial (and emotional) burden of caring for you later in life.

Saving for education has never been easier. There are so many great 529 savings opportunities. As a refresher, a 529 plan is a tax-advantaged savings plan designed to encourage saving for education expenses. These 529 plans are also known as "qualified tuition plans" and are set up by states and authorized by Section 529 of the Internal Revenue Code.

Benefits of 529 Plans[2]

- 529 accounts grow tax free, and distributions used for qualified expenses are not taxed.
- Over 30 states offer tax deductions or credits for 529 contributions.
- The donor typically retains control of the account.
- The beneficiary can be changed to a qualifying family member.
- There are no income restrictions on 529 contributions.

Romantic Fun Stuff—You Can Afford It

We all daydream about traveling the world and whisking our loved ones off on vacations of their dreams. For me, the planning can be as exciting as the actual time in the exotic land. I have also found a great way to turn the planning into an event of its own. Consider setting up a date night or family meeting where the entire agenda for the evening is creating a five-year travel wish list. Plan out details like how often you would like to travel, how much you want to budget, and which destinations you'd like to visit. I hope you have as much fun as my family does organizing and planning our trips.

Retiring to a New Career

I have built quite the list of employees who have come to start their financial planning careers with me after having success in other industries. Recent examples include an engineer, an accountant, a pediatric oncologist, and an accomplished music producer and songwriter (feel free to visit AboundWealth.com to check out our team). All of their career moves have confirmed the need to enjoy what you wake up to do with your life. If you are feeling trapped, consider using your good discipline and savings to reevaluate your career path and build a bridge to a more fulfilling career or to start a new adventure into a field that you have always felt drawn to.

Starting the Real Estate Empire

I am often asked at which stage of the FOO I recommend investing in rental property and real estate. As I have shared many times on my show, real estate should not be viewed as a passive investment. Every investor I have watched create and build wealth through real estate has taken a very active role in that success. Dealing with tenants, whether they are short term (Airbnb or Vrbo) or long term (tenants you sign to a lease), will still be work. Assuming you have the appropriate skills and have done your research on how to navigate real estate appropriately, this is the step in your financial journey when you might consider investing in real estate, now that you have the financial foundation to support your new investment and income stream.

Cash: The Unlikely Wealth Builder

Cash in economic downturns is very valuable. The value of cash goes beyond the peace of mind that it can provide in periods of volatility. Most people do not have any cash on hand or access to more. They're broke. Warren Buffett shared in Berkshire Hathaway's 2004 letter to shareholders, "You only learn who has been swimming naked when the tide goes out."[3]

Without a doubt, most of our neighbors, relatives, and peers are skinny-dipping with their financial lives. They don't have emergency savings and use too much debt. This sets up a unique contrarian opportunity. As cash and liquidity dry up at banks, financial markets enter bear market status and unemployment spikes, creating a moment when purchase prices are disconnected from the intrinsic value of distressed assets. This is the setup to capture once-in-a-lifetime returns if you are the unicorn of the situation—the investor who has excess liquid cash. Here are a few personal examples on why having cash when everyone else is scared and without liquidity can be tremendously valuable:

- October 2008—Apple stock was trading at a price that was not much more than their cash and value of their buildings. It was the opportunity of a lifetime to invest based on future earnings potential and the intrinsic value of the company. After sharing this information with a childhood friend, he purchased approximately $5,000 of Apple. That stock is now worth over $350,000 (he still owns it).

- April 2009—Working with another investor, we purchased two homes from a distressed bank for $256,000 (for both). Those two homes are now worth over $700,000. We knew at the time you could not build those two houses for the price the bank was selling them at. Once again, cash and liquidity was what created the opportunity.
- February 2021—The COVID-19 pandemic had everyone reconsidering what work and life would look like going forward, and the financial and real estate markets were volatile. I used this uncertainty to buy one of the premier buildings on the square of downtown Franklin, Tennessee. It did not take long to know we had done well with our purchase; we received an offer with an immediate seven-figure gain to flip the property after closing. I politely declined the offer, and I have continued to decline ever-growing offers since we closed. Why not sell? This building was a unicorn opportunity, meaning the benefits go beyond looking good on my net worth statement. First, it allows me to turn an existing expense (the rent my businesses pay) into a part of my automatic wealth-building machine. Second, this is a moment to create legacy income. After the notes are paid off, my family will have an income-producing asset beyond my lifetime. Third, the location is exceptional. We all know the biggest rule in real estate is location, location, location. We have that and then some. All of the money in the world, and this is what you would hope you could buy. This type of opportunity only exists when you have liquidity while everyone else is scared and broke.

You too will be able to take advantage of using cash as an unlikely wealth builder if you pay attention to value and keep your eyes open when opportunity presents itself. This is the beauty of wealth building being a long-term journey. Over time, as you work through the FOO, you will have your own opportunities.

Abundance, Flexibility, and Time Are the Fruit

Step 8 is unique because in every other step we focus on the rules and limitations of why you must adhere to that specific financial step. Step 8 is a blank canvas; by this point, you have done what is necessary to be successful, so this step is a checklist that allows you to prioritize and start funding expenses that you will have in the future. You are likely realizing that you won't leave the planet penniless.

If you are reading about Step 8 before achieving this stage in your financial planning, this is a good moment to think ahead about what you hope to do with the freedom you are creating for yourself. This step should empower everyone to think of all options and know how they want to handle this hard-earned freedom. In some respects, it is a bit scary. For many of us, our discipline has defined our success to this point. You reach the top of the mountain and you realize the journey was fulfilling, but you may find yourself feeling far from complete. Money is only a tool, and it is this realization that lets you know you will need to think bigger.

The future expenses we mention here are just a few examples. What might yours be? It's never too early in the journey to start thinking about your "why." What will be your legacy? How do you want to spend your years and resources? If you need inspiration or additional thoughts, don't worry, I have you covered in my chapter on understanding your "why" and the Abundance Cycle.

Download homework at MoneyGuy.com/MillionaireDownloads as you are thinking through what your prepaid future expenses look like. The worksheet will help you determine planning objectives, next steps, financial commitments, and deadlines.

CHAPTER 11

Step 9: Debt Freedom (Prepay Low-Interest Debt)

> The greatest danger for most of us is not that our aim is too high and we miss it, but that it is too low and we reach it.
>
> **—Michelangelo**

Step 9 Preview and What to Know:

You've reached the top, but should you stop? The final step shares an honest look at whether or not you should continue building your wealth or walk into retirement debt free (including your house). Paying off low-interest debt is a controversial topic among financial experts. By exploring how life comes at us each decade and with the use of compelling charts/graphs, I give you the inside scoop to put the finishing touches on your financial masterpiece and have confidence in your debt-free decision.

Aiming to be completely debt free and owning your financial life is a noble cause; the drive to reach full independence, free from obligations and encumbrances, can be intoxicating. Throughout this book I have encouraged you to attack your debt and helped you develop the tools to conquer this wealth-building obstacle. However, there is one exception that we need to spend time on—and there is a reason it is the last step of our journey—and that is prepaying your low-interest mortgage. I want you to be completely without debt by your retirement or financial independence date. However, I do not want you paying off a low-interest mortgage at the expense of building your Army of Dollars, especially while you are in your twenties, thirties, and even early forties. I hope to help you navigate the when, where, and why so you can know you have accomplished all of your financial goals without regrets and are building your best financial life.

If you read, listen, or watch enough financial content, you will quickly realize that financial pundits have very strong opinions about paying down low-interest debt. On one extreme, there are advocates who want you completely debt free as fast as possible. On the complete opposite extreme are those who advocate against paying off any low-interest debt due to the spread (opportunity cost) between what you can earn on your investments versus what you pay in interest.

My approach is more balanced and tied to both the emotion and math of the situation. I want everyone to be debt free as they walk into retirement; it is hard for me to consider you truly financially independent while you have required obligations (debt) on your net worth statement. I am also saddened when I find out that a thirtysomething has missed the opportunity to maximize their Roth IRA or employer-provided retirement plan because they have an unhealthy goal of being completely free of debt by age 40 (or some other arbitrary date).

Mindset by Decade Explained

It may be helpful to narrow the focus and look at healthy financial goals by decade to help you understand the evolution of your mindset and what determines success.

- **Twenties.** The World Is Your Oyster. Seriously, if you are reading this in your twenties, you have the world by its tail. Use this decade to build foundational habits, including:
  - › living on less than you make,
  - › controlling lifestyle creep,
  - › building a strong savings habit,
  - › avoiding the debt trap, and
  - › building the systematic habit of investing through all situations.
- **Thirties.** Surviving the Messy Middle. This is a decade that should be focused on balancing life, career, and wealth building. Your biggest success will be to weather the storm of life and keep the systematic savings and investing habits churning through a busy decade. Much of this success will be through the discipline of not letting your lifestyle expand beyond what it takes to fund your long-term goals.
- **Forties.** It's a Celebration or a Panic Moment. Depending on where you are in the journey, this decade will be a celebration of the skill set of deferred gratification or it will be an exercise in "Where has the time gone?" and "I'd better get to work."
- **Fifties.** Time to Simplify Success or "Oh My Goodness, I Will Be Working Forever." Success creates complication, and as you are looking to embrace freedom you will desire a simpler financial life. Meanwhile, the late comers and procrastinators will

have tremendous doubts about whether or not financial independence is an option, and how they can recover.

Did you catch how this long-term journey may include more conflict than you probably realized? Every decade is going to have its struggles and decisions that will need to be made to not only survive but build on the previous years.

In your twenties, the struggle is primarily an internal battle. There is so much opportunity for success that any little bit of sacrifice is exponentially rewarded in the long term. The thirties are a natural struggle, primarily because of the raw amount of potential life change and the tension that it creates. The forties and fifties are the decades where what you have done previously begins to shine through (or draw attention to the things you haven't done that you should have).

The conflict, struggles, and decisions required to improve your financial situation get harder the older you are when you realize the deficit. There is a reason that midlife crises and marital struggles come to a head in one's forties. Check out this chart on self-reported well-being from PNAS.[1] It's clear to see self-reported well-being drops significantly in the forties and fifties.

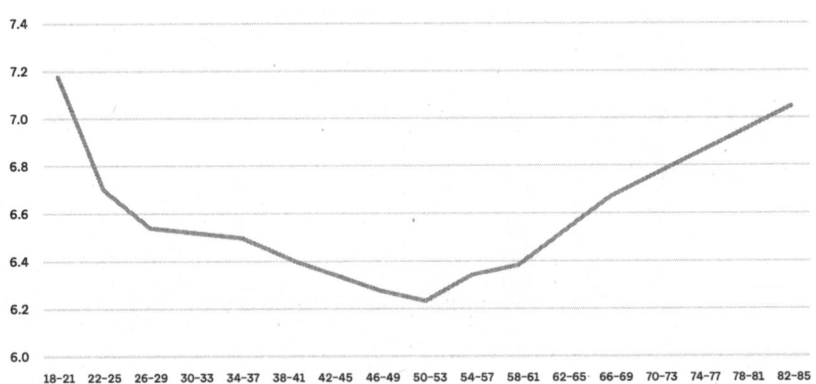

Now compare the ages and happiness to the commitments and obligations of life. From the thirties to the fifties, commitments are at an all-time high while disposable income is stretched thin.

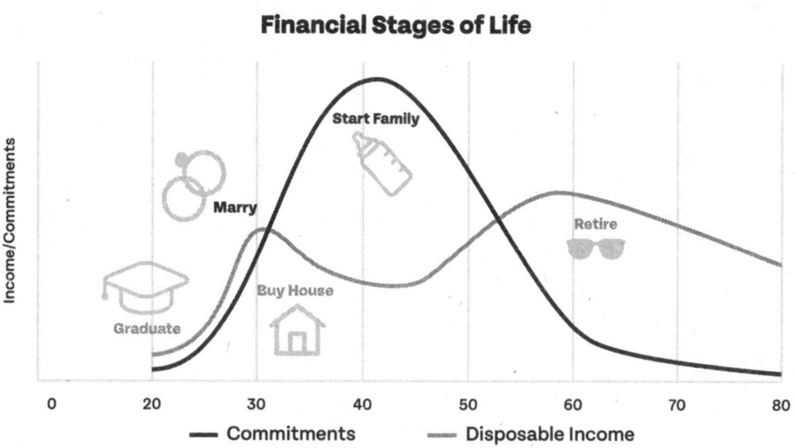

One more chart to add a third source of tension, which you've seen already but it is worth highlighting again. Wealth creation is easiest for those who maximize the resource of time:

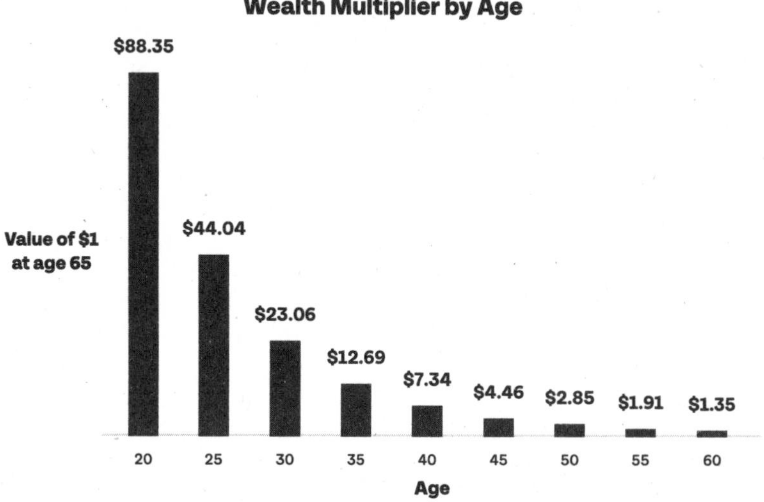

Assumed rate of return is 10% at age 20, decreasing 0.1% each year, reaching a terminal return of 5.5% at age 65.

As you can see from studying these three charts, life is naturally going to be busy, and there are plenty of commitments created through the journey of life (career, marriage, houses, kids, and saving for wealth creation). Investing is most powerful during periods when resources are demanded by other parts of your life, which makes the journey even harder. The optimal way to survive (and even thrive) through such difficult events is to build margin and assets in difficult times, or the early years, and then attack low-interest mortgage debt and obligations in the period of life when you have extra margin of income, and the opportunity cost of lost growth is minimized. Meaning, while you are young, stretched thin on money and time, focus on finding margin and "get wealthy" behaviors, like investing more for retirement. As your Army of Dollars grows and life gets easier, then comes the season to focus on "stay wealthy" behaviors, like paying off low-interest debt.

The Optimized Path

Ready for the big reveal? The easiest way to maximize margin while you are under tremendous stress from life obligations is to utilize traditional 30-year mortgages while you are under 45. This one decision will free you and create extra margin.

First, your 25 percent of gross income toward housing will be maximized with a 30-year mortgage versus the shorter 15-year mortgage. Most of us need a bigger house with more bedrooms and bathrooms while the kids are growing up. By utilizing the guardrail of 25 percent of gross income and the extended 30-year amortization, you will be allowed to buy the larger house you need without derailing your financial life. If you use the same 25 percent guideline with a 15-year mortgage, you may find the larger monthly payment does not offer you the needed margin to buy the house that reflects your current busy life needs. Happiness in the messy middle is a delicate balance between an affordable house and having enough square footage to keep your family from driving you (and each other) crazy.

On the same branch of the tree, I do not want you to prioritize paying down low-interest mortgage debt until you are over 45. This is an optimization strategy to ensure that your Army of Dollars is being maximized while the time component allows compounding interest to work its incredible exponential growth magic. Unless you are already saving and investing 25 percent of your gross income, you should not even sniff around low-interest mortgage debt prepayment. There will be plenty of years in your late forties and early fifties to attack that debt. However, you will never get those years of explosive growth back.

Clarity of Crisis: Strategies to Maximize the Scary Moments

When we share the math difference between investing versus paying down low-interest mortgage debt, there is always a debt crusader who believes a desire to be debt free is superior to taking a more balanced approach. I completely disagree; I grew up in a house where my father was laid off in his early forties after giving twenty-plus years to the same company. Bad things can happen to awesome families, and we should all plan accordingly.

The problem with prepaying your mortgage is that you are putting those dollars into the equity in your home and locking away your easy access to them. The strategy of prepaying only creates a cash flow benefit after the last payment is made. Prior to that point, your capital is very illiquid. The only way to access the money is to refinance or sell the property. Neither option is ideal when bad news tends to travel in packs. For instance, it is not uncommon that you might lose your job while the stock market is getting hammered and the real estate market is soft, which could mean that your home equity could drop right when you would need that asset the most. Fortunately, if you are following the Financial

Order of Operations (FOO), you will have your emergency reserves and, if needed, access to your diversified portfolio. There will always be assets you can access in the worst of times.

Even If Times Are Bad, It Can Be Really Good

A bad period of investing can still be really good news for the long term. Another interesting phenomenon with investing is that even if you are unlucky or really bad at it, you will still be a great investor if your behavior is steady, consistent, and not swayed by all of the bad stuff going on in the world. When I share that volatility and long-term success are strange bedfellows, people are confused; it seems weird to root for a bad year in the market or even a bad decade, but in spite of market downturns, you can still create success.

The Great Depression and the decades that followed weren't particularly banner years for stocks. The market didn't fully recover for over 25 years. You might guess that someone investing during that time period didn't make much money, if they made any at all.

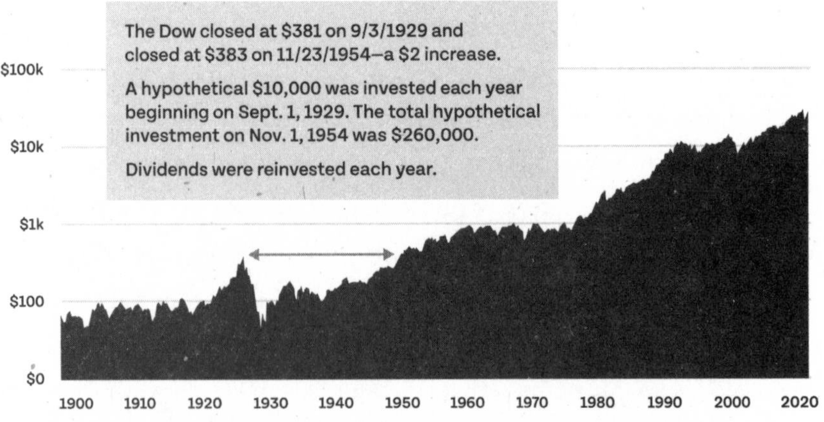

At the end of this 25-year period, the $260,000 investment compounded to $1.5 million, an 11.7% per year total return.

As it turns out, someone investing in the market regularly during that time period would have annualized nearly 12 percent per year, even though the market was flat. That was possible only because of regular, systematic, disciplined investing.

The Great Depression was a long time ago, but this example still holds true over a more recent time period. In the years leading up to and following the Great Recession, beginning in 2007, the stock market was flat for nearly six years. Yet, someone investing $500 per month over this five-and-half-year period would have earned nearly 12 percent annually while the market was flat.

The Market Was Flat for Nearly Six Years . . .

What if you invested $500 per month over this 5½-year period?

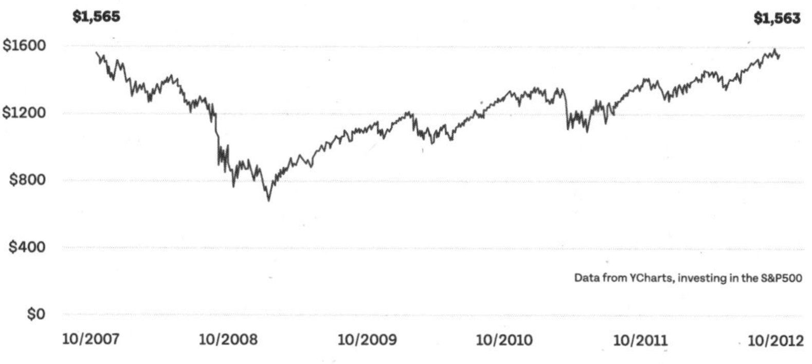

The $33,000 total you invested would be $46,327 by April of 2013.
That's an annualized return of 11.9%.

When we grow that money for 10 more years, from 2013 to 2023, the annualized return is 12.2 percent (without contributing another dollar).

. . . But It Didn't Stay That Way.

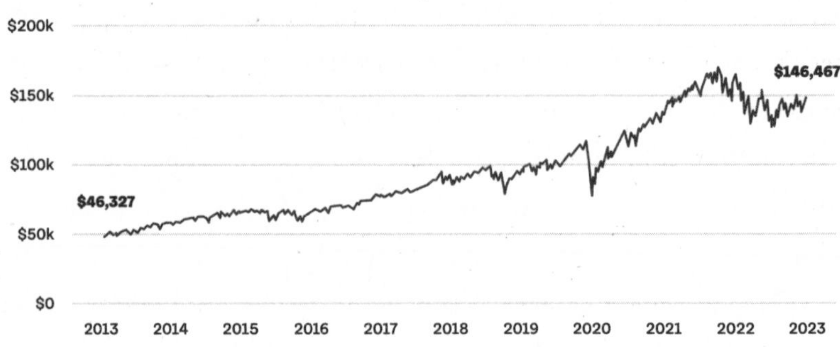

Without contributing another dollar, the $46,327 grew to $146,467 by April of 2023.
That's an annualized return of 12.2%.

Discovering the Beauty of Simplicity in Financial Success

I can remember preparing tax returns in my twenties for people I perceived to be successful. It was so exciting to see the complexities of their taxes, from multiple rental properties, K-1s (tax reporting forms) from different businesses they owned, to completing pages of trades on their Schedule D (Capital Gain/Loss transactions). Looking back on those years, I realize how naïve I was.

Yes, the individuals I worked with were successful, but I can almost guarantee they viewed financial complexity differently than I did as a twenty-something aspiring to build wealth. In my own financial journey, financial complexity has happened naturally. The building of businesses complicated my tax returns. Buying real estate so my businesses could pay rent to me took that tax complication to an even higher level. I now have the tax return that my younger self would have been impressed with, but I also have different goals than twentysomething Brian: I want my financial life to be simpler.

This desire for fewer moving parts came from understanding what creates success and that fulfillment and happiness are not necessarily from money alone. As a result of success, you will find the desire shifts from maximizing wealth behaviors to include behaviors and structures that will allow you to keep your wealth—transitioning from "get wealthy" behaviors to "stay wealthy" behaviors. It is the desire for simplicity and to avoid unnecessary risk that leads you to pursue freedom from all debt. This is what I have found in my own pursuit of personal happiness and success. Since I am now north of the key age of 45, and free to prepay my low-interest debt without regret, I am taking advantage of this opportunity. Yes, I could invest instead of prepaying my low-interest mortgage, but at the end of the day the lost opportunity cost doesn't matter anymore.

At 45, your Wealth Multiplier (what each dollar in the decision would be by retirement) is less than four times, so it is okay to pay off that mortgage. You can also celebrate that you had a road map with the FOO and you followed it through—not to the detriment of your future self, but you made the journey efficiently and in a way that a good leader and general of your Army of Dollars should. Job well done!

Use the checklist that follows to make sure you are prioritizing low-interest debt the right way (and that you are ready to pay down low-interest debts).

Low-Interest Debt Prepayment

☐ **Are you 45 or older?**

If you reach Step 9 of the Financial Order of Operations before age 45, it may be worth thinking twice about prepaying low-interest debt. Your dollars could work harder for you invested, and in some cases having the ability to be debt free is better than actually being debt free. Understand the difference between "get wealthy" behaviors and "stay wealthy" behaviors.

- ☐ **Are you on track for retirement?**
  At this stage of the Financial Order of Operations, having an advisor on your side who can tell you exactly where you stand for retirement is worth considering. Before you prepay any low-interest debt, your retirement should be secure. Consider checking the math with our Know Your Number course at Learn.MoneyGuy.com.

- ☐ **Do you know which debts to prioritize?**
  Not all low-interest debt is created equal. Low-interest student loans and car loans should be prioritized before paying off a mortgage with a similar interest rate. In general, low-interest debt on an appreciating asset, like a house, is a lower priority.

- ☐ **Will you be completely debt free by retirement?**
  No matter when you reach Step 9, we think everyone should aim to be completely debt free by retirement. If you don't think you'll be debt free by retirement, see if you can allocate additional cash flow to paying off low-interest debts.

CHAPTER 12

Understand Your "Why" and the Abundance Cycle

> I hope everybody could get rich and famous and will have everything they ever dreamed of, so they will know that it's not the answer.
>
> **—Jim Carrey**

Congratulations on making it through the Financial Order of Operations! The journey takes years, but knowing that you have a step-by-step path to help navigate all of the oddities and twists and turns of your financial life helps you face whatever may come your way.

Now that you understand the steps to building wealth, you will need to work hard to figure out what your relationship with money is and what powers the motor of your life. Money is nothing more than a tool to help you focus on those things in life that truly matter. The biggest shock for many is that having more money is not the complete solution they had hoped for.

I previously discussed the controversial Princeton study claiming that $75,000 was the amount of income at which emotional well-being stopped increasing, but that is far from happiness and fulfillment. The purpose, and your "why," is what completes the cycle of building happiness and fulfillment. How are your relationships with friends and family? Do you wake up with excitement to work and make the world a better place in your own way? I am not a professional therapist, but I have been around families with money for decades and have learned a few things about human nature and money.

- **We are wired for instant gratification.** Our desire to maximize the moment and load up on instant gratification can lead us astray when it comes to making sound financial decisions. That's why we often struggle with saving for the future or sticking to a budget. Present bias is a real issue.
- **Money can be an emotional roller coaster.** We like to think of ourselves as rational beings, but when it comes to money, emotions can run wild. Whether it's fear, greed, envy, or even the joy of a windfall, we are emotional creatures, and that significantly impacts our financial decisions. Understanding our emotions and how they can manipulate us into bad decisions is crucial for maintaining financial stability and making smart choices.
- **Comparison is the thief of joy.** Social comparison affects our financial decisions. We often gauge our success or failure based on how we stack up against those around us. Grow beyond this mental trap. The only financial journey that matters is your own. Focus on your goals and values and don't let comparisons derail your progress and future success.
- **Losses hurt more.** It's a peculiar quirk of human nature that losses have a greater impact on us than gains of the same magnitude. This phenomenon, known as loss aversion, can influence our risk tolerance and investment decisions. I imagine this served us well in earlier times for survival, but in our modern world you will need to balance this mental struggle.

- **Money can't buy happiness, but it can buy peace of mind.** Having a solid financial foundation allows us to pursue our passions, spend time with loved ones, and have a safety net in case of emergencies. So while money might not bring happiness on its own, it can certainly enhance our overall well-being. There's a well-known quote that many seem to be taking credit for: "I've been poor, and I've been rich. Rich is better!"

I hope that my thoughts and stories have made the journey a bit more real and helped you reflect on what you think about the relationship between money and happiness. It is complicated and nuanced, but in some ways simple.

A big driver of happiness is being deliberate with your time and habits. Settling into good habits takes time, but if you commit to teaching yourself tools for happiness and being productive and efficient, you'll emerge more fulfilled and purposeful. That is what the purpose of the Financial Order of Operations is: to be deliberate with how you spend or invest each dollar. Pay attention to how you make decisions with your time, make long-term decisions, and deploy your Army of Dollars. Do not price yourself out of happiness by being the poorest person on your street or using debt to fake a glamorous life that only exists in your driveway or closet and not in the secret wealth that should reside on your net worth statement. Focus your time and resources on the basics of faith, family, community, and work.

Five Levels of Wealth and Knowing Where You Fall

As you worked through and learned each step of the Financial Order of Operations, hopefully you were able to connect to your own wealth-building path and see how the path is taking shape. If you pull back and take a big-picture view of the journey, you will discover that there are five levels of wealth. As we close out this book, try to determine where you fall in these levels.

Level 1—Stability

At Level 1 wealth, your basics are covered and you can pay your bills. Unbelievably, if you make it through Step 1 of the Financial Order of Operations (FOO) and reach Level 1, you have outperformed the nearly 60 percent of Americans who struggle to come up with $1,000.[1] You know you've successfully reached this level of wealth if:

- You can comfortably pay your bills every month without worrying you'll come up short.
- Your deductibles are covered and cash reserves are building.
- You're insured and protected from premature death and disability.
- You have no credit card debt (paying off cards in full every month).
- You are not walking away from free money (matching funds and Health Savings Account [HSA] dollars).
- Your housing costs are less than 25 percent of your monthly expenses, car payments are inside 20/3/8, your monthly investments are greater than your monthly auto payment, and total debt is less than 35 percent.

Level 2—Strategy

At Level 2, your **Army of Dollars has a plan**—you know you are saving what you should be saving. Less than 48 percent of Americans have three to five months or more of expenses saved in an emergency fund.[2] Only 16 percent of Americans are saving more than 15 percent.[3] At Level 2 of wealth, you are setting yourself apart from these crowds. You'll know you've successfully reached this level of wealth if:

- You have an appropriate emergency fund, are saving for retirement, and are saving for whatever other goals you may have, like buying a house.
- You are saving and investing 20–25 percent of your gross income for the future.
- You are making wealth inevitable by automating as much of your financial life as possible.
- You are living on less than you make to ensure that as your success grows, your Army of Dollars is growing with it!
- You're tracking your net worth and can see year-over-year improvement.

Level 3—Security

At this level of wealth you are no longer sweating the small stuff. You'll know you've successfully reached this level of wealth if:

- You are able to spend money on small, unnecessary expenses without worrying about it. Drinking a latte is not putting you on the naughty list.
- You are continuing to build security and work toward financial freedom.
- You have identified what you value and what brings you purpose, and you are spending your time doing those things.

Level 4—Freedom

This is the level of wealth most people aspire to. At Level 4, you're doing what you want, when you want, how you want. At this point, you've reached financial freedom, giving you the ability to pay for both your current and future needs. You'll know you've successfully reached this level of wealth if:

- Your Army of Dollars can work harder and earn more than you can with your back, brain, or hands. This means your living expenses are no longer tied to your labor. You own your time.
- You are completely debt free. High- or low-interest debt, it does not matter: all debt has been vanquished!
- You live life on your terms and do what you want, when you want, and how you want.

Level 5—Abundance

At this top level of wealth, money doesn't matter anymore. What does matter is that you know who you are, what you value, and what brings you purpose. You are now focused on legacy and looking past yourself to focus on how you make the world better. This is your time to be generous and charitable. If you are successful enough to reach Level 5, it is likely you are "world class" at something. Share that knowledge and wisdom with the heart of an educator. Abundance = Wealth + Purpose.

The Abundance Cycle Does Not End Here

I love the full cycle of abundance. The adage that it is better to give than to receive hits upon something deep within us all. As a kid, I never understood how that saying could ever be true (as I anticipated my next Star Wars toy), but there is something about getting older, more sentimental, and definitely wiser. Being generous has never left me feeling disappointed. It is amazing that the more I have given, the more that my heart and wallet have been replenished.

Over the course of my life, the shine of what money can buy has diminished, and I have found that wealth has allowed me to think beyond myself. This book was written to share what I have learned—both from working with my clients and from my own journey to wealth.

I have found that once I started living between Steps 4 and 5 of the FOO, my focus shifted from what I needed from money to what I could create that is a win-win scenario for me, my employees, and the Money Guy family. The freedom of not worrying about how the basics will get covered has allowed me to expand my investments into projects I believe in, even if monetarily they do not generate a measurable yield. Hiring a producer and content creators to help me expand the voice of *The Money Guy Show* and build focus has been beyond fulfilling. Surprisingly, these investments that weren't intended for financial gain have been yielding tremendous returns.

This brings me to my final thoughts on abundance. Be mindful of where you are in the journey and how you view and use your money and resources. Time is your most valuable and limited resource. It is quite fitting that the most powerful tool in your wealth-building arsenal will also be the one resource you will crave more of. Time moves fast, and fortunately we are designed to create blossoming memories that we get to both take with us and leave behind with our loved ones. Plan accordingly and don't let a day pass without finding a way to make small steps toward your goals, desires, and dreams of what creates fulfillment, purpose, and your "why" for being here.

CHAPTER 13

What I Do with My Money

> What small decision today will maximize this moment and move me closer to my more beautiful tomorrow?

Did you read the entire book? Or have you cheated and skipped ahead to this chapter to get the scoop on what I do with my money? If you read the book, thank you! This was a passion project that has been on my bucket list for the last two decades. After reading exactly what I do with my money in this last chapter, you will see how the core principles and beliefs in earlier chapters shaped my own financial life—a financial life that started at close to zero after college and has expanded beyond my wildest financial dreams. This chapter is meant to be a testimonial that the Financial Order of Operations (FOO) works. That sentence was for those who cheated so you will know to head back to the beginning of the book—the FOO will show you how to build your own wealth.

Life Lessons from My Family

There's a reason the beginning years of childhood are called the formative years. Our experiences and those around us impact our worldview, and that impacts our beliefs, politics, and even how we handle our finances. I have shared throughout this book the events that shaped my life, and I love that this comes full circle with the powerful moment I described earlier in "the Morrow Moment." When I was in eighth grade, before Mr. Morrow lit my wealth-building fire, my father lost his job.

He had worked for McKesson for over 20 years, and the job loss was entirely out of his control. He did not lose his job because he had done anything wrong; he lost his job because McKesson had decided to close down his division completely. This was devastating news to my parents and led to massive changes in the Preston household. He was in his forties, which is hardly the ideal age for someone to need to start over.

During this period of my life, my parents were resourceful, and now, looking back, some of their decisions were actually funny. First, my dad was always a shade-tree mechanic who worked on all of his friends' and neighbors' cars. He was the perfect owner for a fixer-upper. He landed a 1978 Chrysler LeBaron to replace the company car he lost with his job. This was not that small, cute convertible LeBaron of the late '80s. This was a big, hulking, rear-wheel drive version. I have so many great memories of taking that car sideways by slamming on the gas and performing completely stupid burnouts. I shared earlier that your older self will come to understand that your younger self was foolish—this is proof of this concept for me. Dad bought that car for $1,000, drove it for six years, and sold it for $1,200. Just writing this makes me smile, thinking of my dad feeling like he beat the system.

My mom was so tight during this period that we recycled soap. She would collect all of the slivers and remnants of our soaps, melt them together on the stovetop and then let it cool in ice cube trays. In recent years, even my mom admits this was gross and not an efficient use of her time.

For vacations during this lean time, my parents loaded my younger brother and me into a Ford Aerostar van and took us to timeshares because they were free if you sat through a presentation. My dad would negotiate additional incentives. Looking back on this time, I wonder what my parents were thinking. One of the least desirable activities I can think of is sitting through a timeshare presentation, but to my parents, it was a way for us to travel for free. In this light, it was resourceful, too.

I grew up in a house where a dollar was not wasted, and these experiences made me appreciate the value of money. These experiences also demonstrate the power of memories blossoming. Thinking back on this period makes me smile and remember those experiences fondly; the pain of being poor is nowhere to be found. If you asked me what my favorite period of childhood was, it would be this time of scarcity. Why? Because my dad was always around, and this led to incredible memory-building opportunities, such as the awesome weekly Thursday family trip to the grocery store.

There is a tremendous lesson in all this: When it comes to investing, time in the market is more important than timing the market. When it comes to family, time together is more important than the time you work for the expensive expressions of your love. Put the time in, because it is so important!

Marriage, Kids, and the Messy Middle

I was 24 when I got married, and like a complete financial nut, I closed on my first house the month before our wedding date. I believe I broke a few of the rules against making too many life changes in a single year. I am not quite sure why I was in such a hurry to check all of these boxes in life so quickly. The marriage made sense; my wife was way out of my league and I needed to lock her down before she realized the inequality of the relationship. Now, however, buying the house seems like a hurried and forced decision. I think hard-driving, success-seeking individuals often make this mistake because they feel the need to make it through their current phase so they can go on to bigger and brighter opportunities in the next phase. Fortunately, after the house purchase, we slowed down and took the first five years of marriage to learn how to do marriage well, and we even enjoyed the benefits of being childless by traveling and building our own pre-kids history.

My wife and I were very careful to make sure we always built margin into our life to save and invest. The forced automatic savings were increased every year as we received pay raises and bonuses. In retrospect, the majority of our twenties was easy because we were childless, lived in a modest home, and had good jobs that allowed us to save 20 percent easily. Then I started my first business, our first child arrived, and we moved to a larger house, all between the ages of 28 and 31 (that was a busy three years). We dove headfirst into the messy middle.

During the craziness of our early thirties, it felt like we were managing complete chaos. It took three years for my business to grow and create an income that replaced my previous job. Fortunately, I planned ahead and built up 24 months of cash reserves to bridge us through the business start-up. My wife decided not to return to work after our daughter was born. In retrospect, the new house was once again a forced decision, but with a crying baby, you quickly realize the faults with your existing home, like when there are too many stairs between you and the nursery.

I share all of this for one primary reason: Life can be really hard and, in many respects, it will feel like madness sometimes. This is completely normal and you should embrace the messy middle. Focus on what you can control. Build multiple plans to help you navigate the twists and turns. When I made the decision to start a business, I completely restructured our savings and lifestyle. We took fifteen months and lived off of only my wife's salary, and we diverted all savings into cash reserves. That is how we were able to build that bridge that got us through the three years it took to build the business. The minimalism of those years also ensured that our consumption was not burning through the assets and resources we needed to be successful.

This leads to my final point about the messy middle. You do not have to be perfect (or even close) to be successful. You are likely not going to feel comfortable for a number of these chaotic years. Kids, houses, job changes, and life in general can be hard. At the risk of sounding like a country song, the days feel long, but the years are short. Time will fly, so make sure you are enjoying the adventure of this phase. I did not truly feel comfortable financially until my forties. I'm not sure if this confession will be beneficial, but I felt led to share it. I want others to know that all phases will have their own special sweetness but will leave a few cherished scars, too.

How Did All This Impact Me?

My father was really hurt by losing his job. I could sense the regret and anger of having given 20 years of his life to this company only to have a corporate decision upend his entire life and financial success. Aside from experiences like these, life as an adult can be chaos as you add in a spouse, kids, and big life decisions. I internalized what happened to my father and the chaos I encountered in my own messy middle, and it has manifested itself into several strong lessons:

1. **Financial Discipline Is Rewarded.** I knew I wanted to prioritize financial independence by living my life in a disciplined way so that an employer or job could not derail my financial life. A disciplined life does not have to be boring and uneventful. As

my parents demonstrated, and my wife and I embraced, you can have a bedazzled basic life that leaves plenty of room for memories and awesome experiences.

2. **A Big Shovel Helps.** I also knew that I wanted to focus on an occupation that had high earning potential. In college, that desire guided me to major in accounting. I knew I was in the right place when I recognized how many of my fellow classmates' parents were also accountants, and the fact that every graduate of UGA's accounting program had a job lined up by graduation.
3. **Hard-Working Optimists Win.** My work ethic was never going to be questioned. Growing up in scarcity led me to get my first job as soon as I was sixteen and had the independence of transportation. I remember when I realized the positive human element of hard work. My dad took me to help him cut up a tree for firewood. He had me splitting the larger logs, and I was complaining up a storm. He explained that my complaining only made the work take longer and made everyone with us miserable. My father was a disciplinarian, but he also knew how to wield the power of disappointment. The desire to not disappoint my father (who was and still is my hero) flipped a switch, and for the rest of that afternoon, I worked hard to show him what I could do. I was surprised to realize that being busy makes time move faster, and there is no greater feeling than exceeding someone's expectations. My dad heaped praise on me for all of the hard work, and I realized that looking for the positive in situations and working hard was much better than being a pessimistic, lazy complainer. This understanding has helped me throughout my career, and I even manage my employees by looking for those teachable moments that my father provided.

4. **Planning Is Essential.** Where do you want to be and how are you going to get there? If you are not writing down who you want to be financially and creating a system to navigate that path, you are only dreaming. Proper planning helps turn those dreams into reality. Without a plan you are a rudderless ship floating through life, waiting for it all to happen to you. Maximize the tools and system we have shared, including creating net worth statements; managing cash flow and budgeting; and writing down short-term (1–3 years), mid-term (4–7 years), and long-term (> 8 years) goals. If these goals require cash flow planning, like my first business venture did, expand your plan to include three different versions (put on your 3D glasses to gain a better view of the situation):

   a. Down to earth = the "what you think will happen" scenario
   b. Dream becomes reality = the "I am going to be rich" or optimistic scenario
   c. Doo-doo = the complete disaster scenario

   Facing all of the different outcomes will allow you to know what could be coming and how to survive all conditions and outcomes.

5. **Be Thankful, It Goes Fast.** This understanding works in two ways. If someone does something nice or helpful for you, make sure to let them know how much you appreciate their generosity. No matter how talented you are, there are folks in your past who helped you reach your level of success. My business partner, Bo, is a master of this skill, and I have learned a ton from him in this regard. As I have gotten older, I have become more sentimental, which has led me to go on a thank-you tour. I reconnected with my first boss (Bob Kiser) to let him know how much I appreciated his investment in me. It was incredibly powerful because

I had not communicated with him since I put in my notice of resignation in April of 2000. That leads to the second part of being thankful. Don't get so busy that you forget to slow down to take in the blessing of the stage of life you are in. Time is the most valuable wealth builder because if you start investing early, it can propel your financial success beyond your greatest expectations. Time is also the most valuable resource in the world; it is not for sale and only available in limited quantities. We are all leaving this place eventually, so you'd better make sure you are enjoying the journey. Be thankful for what you have and where you are in the journey.

My FOO Journey

Experience creates wisdom, and I do not take for granted the blessing it is to work with successful families and to have the opportunity to learn and apply those lessons to building my own abundant life. What is even better is that I have used those moments to create the FOO and its nine unique steps to building your best financial life. There is a better way to do money, and I get to now share how each has personally impacted my life. Sharing my financial details feels a bit like showing up to the party naked, but I think that it is important for you see how this has developed so you can also know that you too can build your abundant life. My oversharing also allows you to look behind the curtain to see that I eat my own cooking.

Generosity (Financial Mutant Ground Rule #1)

> A generous person will prosper; whoever refreshes others will be refreshed.
>
> **—Proverbs 11:25**

We are built to give, and we are going to unleash the power of paying it forward. For me, the Abundance Cycle does not begin and end with *The Money Guy Show*. I work hard to give a fixed percentage of our income to charity. There is something incredibly powerful about sharing your resources and blessings. Being a Financial Mutant, I have even created a more efficient way to be generous:

- **How Do I Calculate My Fixed Percentage?** My income varies considerably every year and even throughout the year because of my different businesses and fluctuations in the financial markets. To cut through it all, I use last year's income as the guide. I will use my year-end tax projection for the first few months of a year and then true it up when my personal income tax returns are filed.
- **How Do I Give?** I love designing a better mousetrap. My favorite charitable gift is an appreciated asset. It is a win-win situation; I avoid paying income taxes on the gains, receive a tax deduction on the full market value of the donated asset, and my favorite charities get 100 percent of the proceeds. I use Fidelity Charitable to fulfill these goals. There is no minimum to open an account, and grants to charities can be as small as $50. Fidelity does not pay me to share this information, but it is worth disclosing that my Registered Investment Advisory firm Abound Wealth does have a custodial relationship with Fidelity Investments and Charles Schwab. These are the providers we use to work with our financial planning clients.

  Because I am giving appreciated assets monthly out of my Fidelity brokerage account, I am also funding that account with cash and then investing every month. This advanced planning strategy allows me to increase the cost basis and replenish my investment account over time. This strategy is so nerdy that it confirms I am doing what I was put on this Earth to do!

Cash (Steps 1, 4, and 8—Deductibles Covered, Emergency Reserves, and Funding Abundance Goals)

My relationship with cash has had wild swings. I shared earlier the disappointing call I had with my father when I could not cover a few hundred dollars. That is a FOO Step 1—Highest Deductible Covered fail. I continued this journey of building wisdom through experience by relying too heavily on my primary residence equity at the beginning of the 2008 Great Recession (a FOO Step 4—Emergency Reserves fail). That experience scared me, and I have respected the power of having cash, even if interest rates are paltry. I currently have cash reserves that are 14 percent of my liquid investment capital and 4 percent of my total net worth. It is probably worth mentioning that these percentages do not include the cash reserves that I keep in my business accounts; those are on the conservative side too, and there is, on average, enough money in the accounts to cover three to four months of payroll (our biggest expense). When I review the number on paper it looks massive, but it is important to remember that liquidity (cash) is very similar to the oxygen we breathe. We take it for granted until we need it the most.

There are lots of folks who count on me to keep this ship afloat. I know that cash is the safety net that will get my family, businesses, and employees through whatever rough water we may face. As I discussed in Step 8, cash can also be a powerful contrarian wealth-building tool. During the Great Recession, Warren Buffett and Berkshire Hathaway bailed out many struggling companies, including Mars/Wrigley, Goldman Sachs, Bank of America, General Electric, Dow Chemical, and Swiss Re. It was not charity; a 2013 *Wall Street Journal* headline read, "Buffett's Crisis-Lending Haul Reaches $10 Billion."[1] He invested $25.2 billion and made nearly $10 billion in less than five years. What is truly incredible is that much of this was in dividends and premium income, so even after the income, he still owned the shares he purchased at bargain-basement prices.[2] You can make deals of a lifetime if you are ready and the only person with cash when liquidity becomes a scarce resource. Learn from Buffett's example and keep a bit of opportunity capital. This should only occur after you have worked through FOO Steps 1–7, as this is a maximization strategy. Recall how I personally used this strategy when one of the most prominent commercial buildings on the square of downtown Franklin, Tennessee, became available. If I had not kept extra liquidity through the pandemic of 2020, I would not have been able to buy the dream building for my business that will provide a great work environment for Abound Wealth and *The Money Guy Show* for the next decade and will also be a tremendous long-term asset for my family. Cash and liquidity used as an opportunity tool can be very valuable.

I try to maximize what my cash holdings can earn. I use a local bank as my home base. They have my business and personal checking accounts; this allows me to transfer money easily and have a local resource if I ever need to walk down the street and talk to a banker in person. These accounts all stay pretty lean since they do not generate much interest income. The lion's share of my cash reserves are at FDIC-insured online banks and money market accounts in my brokerage accounts. Online banks often like to play games with interest rates. The process of opening and closing accounts is annoying enough to keep me from changing accounts every few months to maximize the interest I can earn on cash. For me, the ideal and most efficient strategy is to bank with institutions that have a history of paying industry-leading rates and are good long-term financial partners. Here are my current online banking relationships (as I write this, I do not have any professional relationships with these banks, meaning they don't pay me to say this):

- Ally Bank—They offer competitive interest rates and other products including car loans and mortgages.
- Fidelity Investments—They offer prime money market funds that are not as safe as FDIC bank accounts but offer yields closer to

treasury rates. These funds also do not have the holding restrictions of buying treasuries and CDs directly.

Employer Plan (Step 2—Max-Out Employer Match)

This is unique because I am both the employer and a participant of the Abound Wealth plan. The intent of Step 2 is to ensure you do not leave a guaranteed 50–100 percent rate of return on the table if your employer offers a healthy match on your employer-provided retirement plan. The 401(k) plan we offer at Abound Wealth does not require our participants to participate in funding their retirement account to receive a 3 percent non-elective contribution. That is guaranteed free money, and those contributions vest immediately for our employees. We then fund another 4–5 percent annually through profit sharing and cash-balance plan contributions. Not a bad deal to receive an 8 percent investment toward your long-term retirement annually from your employer. This also makes it much easier for our employees to reach a healthy investment rate of 20–25 percent of gross annual income.

Personally, I fully fund all of my retirement plans and contribute the most the government allows. The tax benefits are too powerful to ignore. There is a reason the government restricts how much you can contribute and even limits who can participate. Take advantage of this powerful wealth-building tool.

Investing and Creating a Long-Term Wealth Plan

As I am sharing all of this information, I know a number of you are wondering: How do I invest my money? A number of FOO steps require investment decisions (Steps 2, 5, 6, 7, and even 8 with education funding). Here is the big reveal: Over 90 percent of my investment holdings are in low-cost index funds. The exact same guidance that I share on my show, at the firm, with clients, and now in this book is the way I invest my personal money. The remaining is a mix of managed international mutual funds and a few individual stocks.

I do not love buying and selling individual stocks because I find that we humans get too emotionally attached to that company. We deal with executives who have both their human capital (labor and wages) and investment capital all tied up in one company. This is very dangerous because you have all of your eggs in one basket. It could turn into incredible wealth or it could be a cautionary tale of why you need diversification if the stock has an unexpected falling out with the market. If you are going to enter the world of individual stocks, consider keeping the exposure, as a percentage of your total investment assets, low.

Do not outsmart yourself and focus on the wrong behavior that won't help create success. In the beginning, focus your efforts on building a strong foundation through choosing the right education and career and avoiding debt. Use the discipline of how you structure your life so that you work to save and invest 20–25 percent of gross income as fast as possible.

Do not overcomplicate the decision about what to invest in. The vast majority of people could be well served taking advantage of index target retirement funds. Two of the biggest providers of these investment options are Fidelity Investments (Freedom Index Funds) and Vanguard (Target Retirement Funds). These options are great because internal expenses are extremely low, there are no commissions or sales charges, the providers offer easy access to diversified index funds, and they automatically adjust their asset allocation to become more conservative as you approach your targeted date of need.

This single decision will serve you well as you build your Army of Dollars. Once you reach around $500,000 to $600,000 you may find that you desire more. At that point, please do not forget the Abundance Cycle.

Credit Cards (Step 3—Pay Off High-Interest Debt)

I use credit cards but handle them with respect, meaning that I never carry a balance. Credit cards can offer several key benefits, including rewards, extended warranties, purchase protection, and peace of mind while shopping online. There is nothing wrong with using credit cards as long as you do not let them derail your financial life by overspending, carrying a balance, and paying punitive interest. Don't let high-interest debt turn the power of compounding interest against you. Pay off your balance in full before the due date.

I do not mind sharing which credit cards I use, and at the time of writing I was not receiving any compensation for sharing these.

- Costco Anywhere Visa—This card is great for cash back from specific spending categories:
  - Four percent on gas (up to $7,000 per year)
  - Three percent on restaurants and travel
  - Two percent on Costco purchases
  - One percent on everything else
- Disney Visa—This is more emotional than analytical. My family loves what Walt and Roy Disney have created, and my wife requested that we have this card, even though it has a $49 annual fee. Benefits include:
  - Two percent on gas, restaurants, and Disney purchases
  - One percent on everything else
- Fidelity Rewards Visa—This is my catchall card when I do not want to worry about specific spending categories. This card offers 2 percent cash back with no limits. Once again, I feel the need to disclose that my firm uses Fidelity Investments to house client assets. They are not paying me to share this information, but I want to be transparent.

- Amazon Prime Visa—I do not use this card, but I should with as much money as we spend at Amazon and Whole Foods at my house. That is why I am sharing this card since it could be valuable. However, the hassle of unfreezing my credit to apply, and the ongoing account administration, payments, and tracking has me resigned to pass at the moment.
    - Five percent back on Amazon and Whole Foods purchases
    - Two percent back on restaurants, gas, and drug stores
    - One percent on everything else
- American Express Platinum—This is a late addition to my credit card list, and I avoided it for years because it has a high annual fee of $695. However, after I found out that consumer guru Clark Howard had this card in his wallet (when we had him on the show as a guest), I quickly reconsidered. If you are at the level of wealth that you eat and travel well, this is the card for you because it offers many benefits, including access to airport lounges, complimentary (better said: prepaid) breakfast at many higher-end hotels, and reimbursement for common expenses, including digital subscriptions, Uber, and even Global Entry.

Tax-Free Armageddon (Step 5—Max-Out Tax-Free Growth with Roth and HSA)

I absolutely love tax-free growth. Because of that, I use both of these powerful tools. I have been investing in Roth from the beginning (1998). As a result, we have over $700,000 of my household's liquid net worth in Roth assets. I wish that number were higher, but the government restricts how much you can save in these valuable accounts. My income does not allow me to fund Roth IRAs directly, so I have been taking advantage of annually funding my Roth IRA through a Roth conversion strategy.

Every year I fund my Health Savings Account (HSA) with the family contribution limit. I'm still amazed that only 4 percent of HSA accounts take advantage of all three of the triple tax advantage benefits of (1) tax deduction on contributions, (2) tax-deferred growth, and (3) tax-free distribution if used for qualified medical expenses.[3] Anyone who is using an HSA as an annual medical clearing account to pay current-year expenses is only taking advantage of the tax deduction on contributions and tax-free distribution of only the original contribution. What about all of that beautiful tax-deferred growth that can compound exponentially? I encourage you to be part of the 4 percent who use all three of the benefits. Here is an example of the power of these benefits:

My 2020 HSA contribution of $7,100 was invested into an S&P 500 ETF (exchange-traded fund) on March 9, 2020. That investment closed out 2020 up 35 percent. Every bit of my contribution, growth, and eventual distribution will be completely tax free. However, 35 percent is not good enough for me. I plan on letting these dollars continue to grow for at least another ten years. I am diligently keeping records of my qualified medical expenses for each year, and when I feel the time is right, I will submit for a reimbursement. After reimbursement, if there is any money still left in the HSA (there will be), I plan on using it to subsidize my retirement living and medical expenses.

Where do I keep my Roth and HSA accounts? Once again, I use Fidelity Investments to hold and invest these assets.

Max-Out Retirement Options (Step 6)

I shared earlier in Step 2 (Employer Match) that I max-out my Abound Wealth 401(k) annual salary deferrals. In addition to a company 401(k) with a profit-sharing provision, my business partner and I have added a Cash Balance Retirement Plan that allows us to contribute even more dollars to our employees, but that generosity is rewarded with the ability for me to fund even more retirement savings. I share because there will be others who read this book that will be higher-income earners who are desperate to save more for retirement, above and beyond what you can save in a 401(k) with profit sharing. If you resemble that last statement, feel free to make use of the Abundance Cycle and reach out to our firm.

Leverage Hyper-Accumulation (Step 7)—Building That More Beautiful Tomorrow

I've discussed the benefits of saving 20–25 percent of your gross income. If you started investing in your early twenties, you can be closer to 20 percent, and if you got a late start on investing, you will need to save 25 percent or more of your gross income. I calculated my savings and investment rate for last year and it was over 40 percent. That may seem high, but I have quite a few big obligations hanging over me.

First, I have a daughter who, due to autism, will likely never be able to live on her own. That means I will not need to have one retirement funded but two retirements; I am saving for me and my wife (that's one) and then another for my much younger daughter (that's two). Another obligation is my growing business and the employees we will continue to hire. Paying them what they deserve isn't cheap, but I'm happy to do it. In many respects, I am living and saving for lives outside my own. In addition to saving for my daughter's future, saving for goals like purchasing buildings or hiring more employees fulfills my dream of growing the business and impacting more folks. It is tremendously fulfilling to watch my employees get married, buy houses, have children, and buy cars. I feel like the businesses I created are helping them reach their own goals, and it provides me purpose and fulfillment.

Your purchase of this book and support for everything else that comes from *The Money Guy Show* is a big part of this goal. Thank you for making this all possible. Not to get too sentimental, but I have always felt that I was blessed with all of this because God knew that I would have large needs with my daughter. Thank you again for being part of this incredible journey and making this all possible.

Prepay Future Expenses—Funding Abundance Goals (Step 8)

I contribute to several accounts for future expenses. They did not start all at once. I started with the education goals first when my daughters were born, and then I layered in the other accounts as success allowed me to be more generous with my planning goals.

- **529 savings plans.** I have consistently added to my daughters' 529 accounts for much of their childhoods, and it is amazing to see how these accounts have grown. We have been able to send my oldest to college without much stress to our financial household. We will likely transfer my youngest daughter's 529 to her ABLE account (see below) at some point. For each of their 529 plans, I chose the aggressive age-based investment option. Both of the plans are still invested in the Georgia 529 plan because when we lived in Georgia there was a very good state tax deduction for contributions. Tennessee, where we now live, does not have a state income tax on individuals, so there did not seem to be a big enough reason to move the assets to another plan. In addition, Georgia is one of those states that penalizes you if you try to move 529 assets to an out-of-state plan after taking advantage of a deduction on your Georgia tax returns.
- **Custodial accounts.** Having two daughters, I was concerned about wedding costs. From early ages I set up custodial accounts that I initially funded with $100/month and, at some point, I increased that to $200/month for each of my daughters. I know you will be shocked—they are invested in index target retirement funds (are

you noticing a trend?). Custodial accounts allow you to contribute to an investment account in your child's name and lower tax bracket. The accounts are very flexible and can be used for education, weddings, or even help with a first home down payment. The downside is that your child will own and control these assets as of the age of majority in your state. I am hopeful that I have taught my daughters well and that they will use the money wisely.

- **ABLE account.** ABLE accounts are tax-advantaged savings accounts for individuals with disabilities; visit the ABLE National Resource Center at ablenrc.org for some great ABLE account resources. I am fortunate that the state of Tennessee has been very proactive in being a leader in ABLE accounts. I have been funding my youngest daughter's ABLE account to the contribution limit each year. When you have a child with special needs, you have fears about what will happen when you are no longer here. I know it is a scary subject, but I am working hard to make sure that she is well funded, and the plan is there so she will always know how much she was loved and how well her future was planned for.

Prepay Low-Interest Debt (Step 9)—Debt Freedom

I currently have 83 percent equity in my house. That is very healthy, and it is great that the debt on my house is only 17 percent of what the house is worth. However, I am officially at the age that I want my financial life simplified. My goal is to have the remaining debt paid off soon. The mortgage is my only personal debt. We do not have debt on our vehicles, and credit card debt does not exist in my house.

When I say low-interest, it is *really* low-interest. I refinanced into a 2.5 percent 15-year mortgage in 2020. That money is so cheap that it has led to numerous lunch discussions with my business partner, Bo. Bo picks on me for being bad with math and wanting this debt paid off when my FDIC savings accounts are paying more than 2.5 percent. Bo is not wrong; if I invested or even kept in cash the money I am planning to use to prepay my mortgage, I would likely do much better and build even more wealth.

I am at the level of wealth where maximization is no longer the only objective whispering in my ear. I now have the goal to simplify and minimize as many risks as possible in my life. The journey consists of building wealth, but there is also the component of keeping your wealth. All the years of saving and investing have built a level of investment assets that grow more than I make in earned income most years. This is a big indicator that I am at financial independence.

The compromise and solution that Bo and I have worked out from all of our lunch discussions is that I am going to invest that additional money instead of just sending extra principal payments each month, with the goal that in the next few years I will write a check from the proceeds of my portfolio assets to pay the house off in full. To me it is a win-win situation, and it doesn't hurt that I am rounding up my monthly payment because I am not a minimum-payment type of Financial Mutant!

Questions That Have Served Me Well

As this book draws to a close, I felt that in addition to helping you create your personal financial road map and action plan, I could also assist you with context and perspective. It is always important to make sure your perspective and field of vision are not clouded and that there are no blind spots that are keeping you from making the best decisions. Here are the questions that have helped me gain a clear view as I navigate through life:

Am I Challenging Myself Enough?

There is great value in enjoying the moments when everything seems to be going well. However, it is equally important to pause during these times and assess whether we are truly pushing ourselves for personal growth. Are we challenging ourselves to reach our full potential? Example: I was a finance major at UGA. I questioned if the major was going to bear fruit because at that moment in time, I noticed that many folks with a finance major ended up in sales positions, selling products to people they already knew or struggling to find their first job out of college at banks and brokerage firms. That path didn't seem right for me because I did not have wealthy family or friends to market to. So I decided to challenge myself and make a bold move. I switched my major to accounting, knowing full well that it would come with greater challenges and uncertainties. It wasn't an easy decision, but I knew deep down that it would set me up for a more successful future. There is even the famous quote: "Fortune favors the bold." That's what this question is all about: challenging yourself and making hard decisions today that will pay off in the long run. Sometimes, what may seem like a difficult choice in the moment can lead to significantly larger rewards down the road. It's about envisioning your desired future and having the courage to take action. It's in those moments of discomfort and growth that we pave the way for a brighter and more beautiful future.

Are You Willing to Do What Others Are Not?

The road less traveled only becomes a shortcut if you are willing to do the work of navigating the path that others avoid. Example: I landed my first CPA job not because I had the best grades or the best interview. It was because I took that extra step, the one that most candidates overlook. Before my on-site interview, I reached out and interviewed one of the firm's clients. I then made sure I mentioned that in a subtle way to each of the partners who interviewed me. This small act made a significant impact. The partners later revealed that out of hundreds of candidates, I stood out because I was the first prospective employee who had ever taken that extra step. I became the peacock among my peers, and it gave me a distinct advantage. Being willing to go above and beyond, to stand out from the crowd, can have its advantages. It's about embracing the mindset of being unique and doing what others may overlook. It's about finding those opportunities to shine, even in subtle ways, and showcasing your commitment to excellence.

Is There Good from This Bad Situation?

Life has a way of throwing curveballs at us, but I've always believed that even in the midst of bad situations, there's an opportunity for something good to emerge. It's all about embracing a contrarian mindset, flipping the script, and finding the silver lining. The passing of my father was one of the most difficult times I've ever experienced. Yet, even in that dark moment, I made a conscious decision to extract something positive from the pain. I used it as a catalyst to refocus my life, to truly understand what I valued and what was important to me. That exercise of introspection and soul-searching pushed me to step out of my comfort zone and take a leap of faith. I left my comfortable job and embarked on the journey of starting my first business. It was a bold move, but one that aligned with my newfound clarity and purpose. Looking back, I can confidently say that it was a turning point that set me on a path of fulfillment and personal growth. Another twist was the COVID-19 pandemic. While it brought countless challenges and hardships, I saw an opportunity amid the chaos. With extra time on my hands, I decided to embark on a new endeavor, writing this book. It was a chance to share my knowledge, experiences, and insights with others, and hopefully inspire them to navigate their own financial journeys. The lesson here is to always keep an eye out for the silver linings, even in the darkest of times. It's about shifting our perspective—embrace the power of reframing and remember that the most significant breakthroughs often emerge from the most challenging moments. Life is a journey filled with ups and downs, but it's how we respond to those lows that truly defines us. Stay resilient, stay open to the lessons, and keep searching for the silver linings.

Who Cares What the Popular Kids Are Doing?

The moment we stop worrying about what the so-called popular kids are doing, we open ourselves up to finding our own authentic path to fulfillment. It's about breaking free from the trap of comparison and embracing our individuality, regardless of what the herd may think. Let me share an example from my own life that exemplifies this. Back in 2005, when I bought my first iPod and discovered the world of podcasts, I was captivated. The idea of creating my own digital classroom, a platform for education and sharing knowledge, ignited a fire within me. Now, you might think this was a nerdy pursuit, and you know what? It was, but I didn't care. My wife felt the need to caution our close friends against poking fun at my new hobby. Being a bit different and having a vision that others may find odd turned out to be a blessing. It allowed me to pave my own way and build something meaningful. Little did I know that this seemingly nerdy pursuit would change the world of personal finance. The truth is, when we embrace our uniqueness and follow our passions, amazing things can happen. We break free from the need to keep up with the broke Joneses and seek validation from others. We become the contrarians who chart our own course, unconcerned with the opinions of the herd. Here's a secret for all the insecure teenagers out there: The cool kids? They're insecure too. So why waste your time trying to fit into a mold that doesn't truly reflect who you are? Embrace your inner nerd, your unique interests, and your vision for the future. Trust me, nerds tend to win in the long run.

Am I Gracious and Thankful to Others?

One of the simplest yet most profound principles in life is the golden rule: treating others the way you want to be treated. It sounds so straightforward, but its impact can be truly life changing. At the core of this principle lies the practice of graciousness and thankfulness—a grace-filled heart that forgives easily and expresses gratitude often. Let me share an example that highlights the power of gratitude in action. My business partner and co-host of *The Money Guy Show*, Bo Hanson, possesses a remarkable talent for saying thank you. I've never met anyone who expresses gratitude as sincerely and generously as Bo does. Whether it's a meal he didn't have to pay for or any act of generosity, he goes above and beyond to express his heartfelt appreciation. What I've witnessed firsthand is that Bo's exceptional skill of expressing gratitude has been a catalyst for his journey from poverty to abundance. It's a testament to the truth that when we cultivate a spirit of gratitude and acknowledge the generosity of others, it paves the way for even greater acts of generosity in our own lives. I often share this wisdom with my daughters, emphasizing that mastering the art of saying thank you can unlock a world of abundance and goodwill. It's a valuable lesson that transcends financial success; it's about fostering meaningful connections and nurturing a spirit of appreciation. Saying thank you is not just a mere formality; it's an invitation for more blessing to flow into our lives.

What Small Decision Today Will Maximize This Moment and Move Me Closer to My More Beautiful Tomorrow?

It's truly awe inspiring to witness how big achievements can snowball from small decisions. I firmly believe that the small choices we make today have the potential to shape our destiny. Yet these decisions are often influenced by the whispers of our inner voice during quiet moments. Controlling and directing that inner voice is a crucial aspect of building success. Life is filled with doubters and negative voices, but if we don't believe in ourselves, who will? Doubt can quickly lead to failure. Sadly, the majority of Americans classify themselves as pessimists, but we have the power to reframe our inner voice and embrace an optimistic perspective. By cultivating an inner optimist, one who believes in making small positive decisions each day, we unleash an unstoppable force that propels us toward our dreams. Our research on millionaires has shown that 84 percent of them classify themselves as optimists. This optimistic outlook fuels their success and their belief in making their dreams a reality through consistent, small, positive steps. Controlling our inner voice also helps us avoid feeling overwhelmed by the complexity of our goals. When we focus on small but positive steps forward, we prevent ourselves from being consumed by the multitude of variables and potential obstacles that could overwhelm us if considered all at once. Reflecting on my own journey, I realize that setting simple goals allowed me to manifest much larger and more intricate goals over time. When I started my first business, I had no idea about the compliance challenges across multiple states, the substantial software expenses, or the responsibility of providing opportunities to a team of 30 employees. If I had known all these complexities from the beginning, I might have faltered at the starting line. Instead, the purity and simplicity of my initial aspirations—to educate clients, spend more time with family, and contribute to my community—guided me through the small but important steps. So take a moment to write down what you want to accomplish. Embrace the simplicity of small, positive steps, for they will lead you along the path less traveled, where greatness awaits. Your journey to financial success and personal fulfillment begins with the small decisions you make today, for they hold the potential to unlock and create your more beautiful tomorrow.

Unleashing Your Financial Potential

To support your ongoing growth and motivation, we have developed an entire platform of content (*The Money Guy Show*). It's a treasure trove of valuable resources that will keep you on track and fuel your financial progress. Dive into our podcast episodes, explore our courses, engage with our YouTube channel, and access a wealth of free resources on MoneyGuy.com. This platform is designed to ensure your financial education remains dynamic and ever evolving.

Now that you've reached the end of this book, it's time to embark on the journey of action. Remember to cherish the blossoming memories along the way, find joy in each stage of your financial progress, and lean into the wisdom that propels you to the fifth level of wealth. This is where you truly understand who you are, what you value, and what brings you purpose.

You possess all the tools you need to become the commander of your Army of Dollars. It's time to build a life that goes beyond common sense and maximizes all of your potential. Embrace the best version of yourself and live in the abundance that awaits!

Acknowledgments

This book was not a solo endeavor and journey. I want to thank my family for always believing in my dreams, specifically, my wife, Jennifer, for not thinking it was crazy that I wanted to leave my stable job after my father passed away to start my own planning business, and for asking my friends to go easy on me when I started my nerdy hobby of podcasting before anyone even knew what that was.

I'd like to thank my mom (Pam) and dad (Big John) for modeling for me what a loving husband-and-wife relationship looks like and how to not take a single dollar for granted. My father passed away from leukemia in 2000, and I ponder what he would think of what I have been blessed with. He is a big part of who I am and was also a tremendous influence on my friends and anyone else who had the pleasure of knowing him. His passing is what nudged me to redefine what I was doing with my life and to build something that would allow me to be the father he was and bless clients and those who worked with me. Little did I know this win-win foundation was the beginning of the Abundance Cycle.

You never know what day at work or decision will change your life. Little did I know when I interviewed a young Bo Hanson at the University of Georgia that one day we would be business partners and he would be the wind at my back to keep pushing me to stretch those goals and dream bigger. I have so many stories I could share that would detail that Bo is decades wiser than his physical age and a tremendous spiritual amplifier, too.

I am so thankful that Rebecca (Rebie) and Daniel have joined the content team. Rebie's parents should have had twenty-six children, because she is incredible at keeping me and Bo motivated and pushing forward while still being a spectacular human being. Daniel is that quiet friend who lets his work speak for him. This book would likely have less than ten commas without Daniel's help and edits.

Thank you to my literary agent, Bryan Norman. Without you I would still be googling publishing legal terms and wasting time on matters that I had no business dealing with. I brag about my awesome agent to anyone who will listen. I am so happy that it was in a meeting with you and Rebie that we had our eureka moment on the title *Millionaire Mission*.

Thank you to Matt Holt and the BenBella team. Matt wowed me with his excitement for my vision. The team has been flexible, patient, and open to our suggestions and opinions.

Thank you to everyone who found my podcast or YouTube videos and came on this journey with me. I share so passionately because I do feel that we are part of something that can change lives. Thank you to all of Abound Wealth's clients; you are the engine that has supported and allowed this passion project to keep speed. This message needs to be shared so that others can find the abundance that *The Money Guy Show* has created for our audience and my family and co-workers. Thank you for the years of support, and here's to many more years of success.

Appendix

Download all resources mentioned in the book at MoneyGuy.com/MillionaireDownloads. We believe that these resources are best when downloaded and printed or viewed on a computer, but in the following pages you can see previews of what to expect.

What's Your Money "Why"?

Understanding your relationship with money and what drives your financial decisions is an important step toward achieving a healthy relationship with wealth-building and the tool of money. Here are important questions to ask yourself to understand better where you are starting in your personal Millionaire Mission.

1. **What are you hoping to achieve from reading this book?**

   List specific goals, learning objectives, or insecurities you'd like to overcome.

2. **Do you get more enjoyment from spending or from saving/investing?**

   Is there a specific reason from your past that is influencing this behavior?

3. **What are your three greatest financial fears and concerns?**

   Are any of these fears mitigated with knowledge and good financial planning?

4. **If you had unlimited financial resources, what would you do more of or buy more of?**

   What about this action or item brings you happiness/satisfaction?

5. **What does "wealthy" look like to you?**

You will be surprised how much this changes over your lifetime. Please provide specifics, including dollar amounts, deadlines/time, career objectives, and lifestyle indicators.

6. **What are your biggest financial mistakes or regrets?**

Describe your greatest financial setbacks or mistakes. Why do you regret them? What do you wish you would have done differently? How did it change how you think about money?

7. **What are your top financial goals?**

Make these goals SMART: Specific, Measurable, Achievable, Relevant, and Time-Bound.

8. **Time Machine Exercise!**

Write down what success looks like at different points in the future.

12 MONTHS:

5 YEARS:

10 YEARS:

Step 1—$200-a-Month Challenge

How it works: Use the table below to help you spot areas you may be able to cut expenses. Enter the amount saved per month by cutting expenses in the "Amount Saved" column. Complete the $200 challenge by saving at least $200 per month!

Savings Opportunity	Amount Saved
Ungrateful Service Providers Many service providers give new customers better rates than loyal customers. Look at auto and homeowners insurance, utilities, mobile phone, and more.	
Weekly Cashflow Leaks Any little "extras" of life that you buy out of comfort or convenience rather than necessity go here, including things like coffee and eating out.	
Subscriptions It seems like almost everything is a subscription these days. Try cutting out some subscriptions, like streaming services, online games, and intro offers.	
Pantry Audit How much of your pantry is made up of junk food you can take a break from, and how many items are you rebuying because you forgot you already had one?	
Anything Else? Use this space for any other savings not listed above. There have been seasons of life where we paused convenient expenses, like landscaping or housekeeping.	
TOTAL MONTHLY SAVINGS:	

Step 2—Wealth Multiplier

How Powerful Is Your Army of Dollar Bills?

Here's the mathematical breakdown of what every single dollar invested could turn into by age 65. See how much you need to be investing to reach $1 million invested by retirement.

Age	Wealth Multiplier	Monthly Investment*	Age	Wealth Multiplier	Monthly Investment*
20	**88.35**	**$95**	43	5.41	$1,454
21	76.56	$109	44	4.91	$1,620
22	66.48	$125	**45**	**4.46**	**$1,806**
23	57.84	$142	46	4.06	$2,014
24	50.42	$162	47	3.71	$2,248
25	**44.04**	**$184**	48	3.39	$2,512
26	38.54	$209	49	3.10	$2,812
27	33.80	$236	**50**	**2.85**	**$3,155**
28	29.70	$267	51	2.62	$3,549
29	26.14	$302	52	2.41	$4,006
30	**23.06**	**$340**	53	2.23	$4,541
31	20.39	$383	54	2.06	$5,176
32	18.05	$430	**55**	**1.91**	**$5,938**
33	16.02	$483	56	1.78	$6,871
34	14.25	$541	57	1.65	$8,038
35	**12.69**	**$606**	58	1.54	$9,538
36	11.33	$678	59	1.44	$11,537
37	10.14	$757	**60**	**1.35**	**$14,333**
38	9.08	$845	61	1.27	$18,523
39	8.16	$943	62	1.19	$25,498
40	**7.34**	**$1,052**	63	1.12	$39,436
41	6.62	$1,172	64	1.06	$81,216
42	5.98	$1,306	**65**	**1.00**	**$1,000,000**

Expected lifetime return for ages 0 to 20 is 10% per year, decreasing by 0.1% each year after 20. All dollar values rounded to the nearest whole dollar.

Step 4—Expenses Worksheets

You should typically have between 3 and 6 months' worth of expenses in an emergency fund, depending on your job security, career field, and other factors. Before you can know how much you should have, you must know how much you are spending every month. Use the following worksheet to tabulate your expenses.

To begin, what is your monthly gross household income?

FIXED EXPENSES

Fixed expenses are necessary expenses that are the same every month.

CATEGORY	DESCRIPTION	MONTHLY COST	% OF MONTHLY INCOME
Housing			
Savings			
Charitable Giving			
Internet			
Phone			
Auto Insurance			
Life Insurance			
Other Insurance			
Loan Repayment			
Other			
Other			
	Total Monthly Fixed Expenses		

VARIABLE EXPENSES

Variable expenses can change from month to month, and some months they may even be zero. Estimate your variable expenses below.

CATEGORY	DESCRIPTION	MONTHLY COST	% OF MONTHLY INCOME
Household			
Clothing			
Groceries			
Auto Expenses			
Utilities			
Other			
	Total Monthly Variable Expenses		

DISCRETIONARY EXPENSES

Discretionary expenses vary from month to month and they aren't necessary to live.

CATEGORY	DESCRIPTION	MONTHLY COST	% OF MONTHLY INCOME
Dining Out			
Entertainment			
Subscriptions			
Technology			
Add'l Savings			
Other			
	Total Monthly Discretionary Expenses		
	TOTAL MONTHLY EXPENSES		

To cover all of your monthly expenses, you need an emergency fund between

________ and ________

for 3 to 6 months' worth of living. Nobody knows you better than you do. If you think you will cut back on discretionary expenses if you lose your job, you may only need to cover your fixed and variable expenses.

MONEY GUY REMINDER

Covering 3–6 months of expenses is only a general rule of thumb. There are situations in which it makes sense to maintain a larger emergency reserve, like if you are in a unique field or if you are solely dependent on one source of income. For example, when entering retirement, consider having 18–36 months of expenses covered in your emergency reserves.

Step 5—Roth and/or HSA Contributions

A **ROTH IRA** is an individual retirement account where you can set aside after-tax income for your future. Withdrawals can be made tax free after age 59½.

An **HSA**, or Health Savings Account, is an account designed for high-deductible health plan participants to cover out-of-pocket medical expenses. It may also be used as a retirement savings vehicle.

The younger you are, the longer your dollars have to grow. Roth IRAs are especially powerful because all that growth will be tax free if taken in qualified distributions. HSAs are tax deductible when you contribute, savings grow tax free over time, and withdrawals used to pay for qualified medical expenses are tax free.

HSA ELIGIBILITY

1. Review your current health insurance plan.
   a. Does your plan have a deductible of at least $1,600 (or $3,200 for a family)?*

      ☐ **Yes** ☐ **No**

   b. Are maximum out-of-pocket expenses $8,050 ($16,100 for a family) or less?*

      ☐ **Yes** ☐ **No**

ROTH IRA ELIGIBILITY

2. Are you eligible to contribute to a Roth IRA?
   a. Is your adjusted gross income (AGI) less than $138,000 ($218,000 for those married filing jointly)?

      ☐ **Yes** ☐ **No**

   b. Are you age 50 or older?

      ☐ **Yes** ☐ **No**

If you are under the income thresholds ($138,000/single, $218,000/married filing jointly), you may be eligible to make the maximum contribution to a Roth IRA. If you are under 50, you can contribute $7,000 in 2024, and if you are 50 or older, you can contribute $8,000 in 2024.

If you aren't eligible to make the full contribution, use the flowchart on the following page to determine whether you can use the Roth IRA conversion strategy to make the maximum contribution.

*Numbers valid for 2024, but may change in future years.

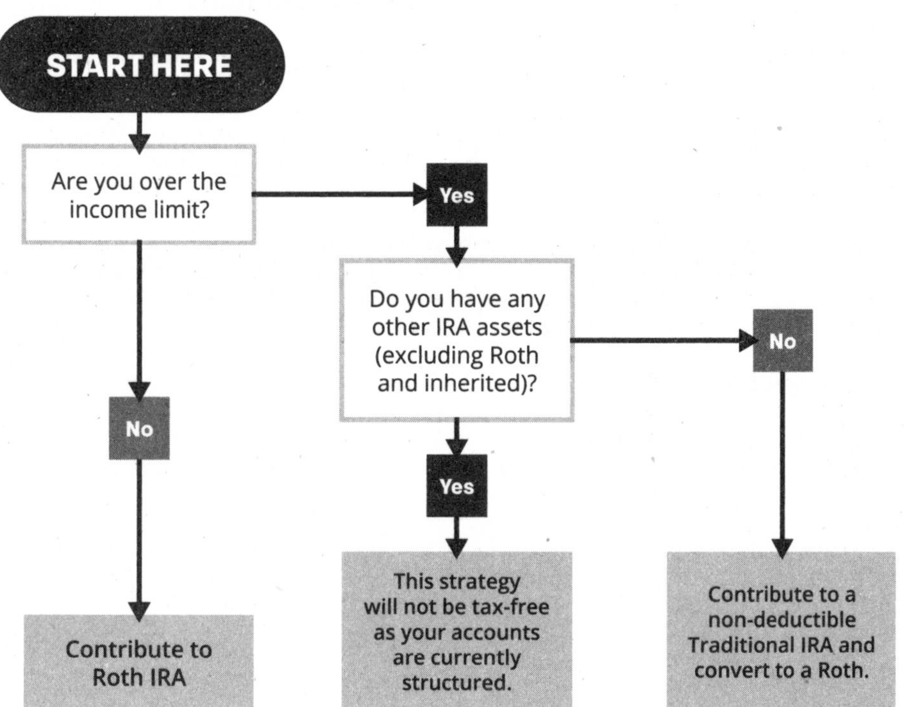
START HERE
Are you over the income limit?
Yes
No
Do you have any other IRA assets (excluding Roth and inherited)?
No
Yes
Contribute to Roth IRA
This strategy will not be tax-free as your accounts are currently structured.
Contribute to a non-deductible Traditional IRA and convert to a Roth.

Step 6—Net Worth Statement

CURRENT YEAR

ASSETS		Jane	John	Titled Jointly	Total Capital by Segment	% of Total Assets by Segment
CASH					$60,000	4.86%
	CHECKING ACCOUNTS			$15,000		
	SAVINGS ACCOUNTS	$10,000		$25,000		
	HSA	$5,000				
	CD		$5,000			
INVESTMENTS					$300,000	24.31%
After-Tax	BROKERAGE ACCOUNTS	$25,000	$80,000			
After-Tax	ESPP*		$2,000			
After-Tax	RSU†	$8,000				
After-Tax	OPTIONS	$12,000				
Tax-Deferred	401(K)		$60,000			
Tax-Deferred	403(B)	$20,000				
Tax-Deferred	SEP-IRA		$20,000			
Tax-Deferred	ROLLOVER IRA	$40,000				
Tax-Free	ROTH IRA	$8,000				
Tax-Free	ROTH 401(K)	$20,000				
Tax-Free	HSA		$5,000			
BUSINESS INTERESTS					$50,000	4.05%
	CONSULTING	$50,000				
PROPERTY					$824,000	66.77%
	PRIMARY RESIDENCE			$800,000		
	AUTOMOBILE #1			$12,000		
	AUTOMOBILE #2	$8,000				
	ART/COLLECTIBLES		$4,000			
TOTAL ASSETS		$206,000	$176,000	$852,000	$1,234,000	100%

*Employee Stock Purchasing Program

†Restricted Stock Units

LIABILITIES	Jane	John	Titled Jointly	Total Capital by Segment	% of Total Assets by Segment
LIABILITILES				$800,000	64.83%
AUTO LOAN #1			$10,000		
CREDIT CARD DEBT	$5,000				
MORTGAGE			$700,000		
STUDENT LOANS	$20,000	$65,000			
DEFERRED TAXES				$15,000	1.22%
CAPITAL ASSETS	$15,000				
TOTAL LIABILITIES	$40,000	$65,000	$710,000	$815,000	66.05%

NET WORTH	**$419,000**

Step 8—Prepaid Future Expenses Worksheet

Prepaid future expenses is the stage where you save for your kids' college, rental property, extravagant vacations, and maybe that cabin in the mountains. Use the space below to fill in your prepaid future savings goals and your "why" behind each one.

1. Planning objective: ______

   Next step: ______

   Financial commitment: ______

   Deadline for goal: ______

2. Planning objective: ______

   Next step: ______

   Financial commitment: ______

   Deadline for goal: ______

3. Planning objective: ______

   Next step: ______

   Financial commitment: ______

   Deadline for goal: ______

4. Planning objective: ______

   Next step: ______

   Financial commitment: ______

   Deadline for goal: ______

Notes

Introduction

1. "Personal Saving Rate." FRED, September 29, 2023. https://fred.stlouisfed.org/series/PSAVERT.
2. Dilworth, Kelly. "Average Credit Card Interest Rates: Week of August 2, 2023." CreditCards.com, August 3, 2023. https://www.creditcards.com/news/rate-report/.
3. Gillespie, Lane. "Bankrate's Annual Emergency Fund Report." Bankrate, June 22, 2023. https://www.bankrate.com/banking/savings/emergency-savings-report/.
4. Stanley, Thomas J. and William D. Danko. *The Millionaire Next Door: The Surprising Secrets of America's Wealthy*. New York City, New York: Pocket Books, 1996.
5. Clark, Jeffrey W. "How America Saves Report 2023." Vanguard, 2023. https://institutional.vanguard.com/content/dam/inst/iig-transformation/has/2023/pdf/has-insights/how-america-saves-report-2023.pdf.
6. Clark, "How America Saves Report 2023."
7. Urban, Tim. "The Artificial Intelligence Revolution: Part 1." Wait But Why, July 18, 2023. https://waitbutwhy.com/2015/01/artificial-intelligence-revolution-1.html.

Chapter 1

1. "Spiva: S&P Dow Jones Indices." SPIVA | S&P Dow Jones Indices, June 30, 2023. https://www.spglobal.com/spdji/en/research-insights/spiva/#.
2. Duvall, James. "Trends in the Expenses and Fees of Funds, 2019." Investment Company Institute, March 2020. https://www.ici.org/doc-server/pdf%3Aper26-01.pdf.

Chapter 2

1. Gillespie, Lane. "Bankrate's Annual Emergency Fund Report." Bankrate, June 22, 2023. https://www.bankrate.com/banking/savings/emergency-savings-report/.
2. "Residential Fire Estimate Summaries." U.S. Fire Administration, April 28, 2022. https://www.usfa.fema.gov/statistics/residential-fires/index.html.
3. "Brief History." Insurance Information Institute, May 1, 2014. https://www.iii.org/publications/insurance-handbook/brief-history.

Chapter 3

1. Alling, Brian T. and Jeffrey W. Clark. "How America Saves 2021." Vanguard, 2021. https://institutional.vanguard.com/content/dam/inst/vanguard-has/insights-pdfs/21_CIR_HAS21_HAS_FSreport.pdf.
2. Grant, Kelli. "1 in 5 Workers Misses Out on This Free Money for Retirement." CNBC, July 6, 2017. https://www.cnbc.com/2017/06/28/missing-the-employer-match-could-hurt-your-retirement-goals.html.
3. "The National Study of Millionaires." Ramsey Solutions, April 12, 2023. https://www.daveramsey.com/research/the-national-study-of-millionaires.
4. Clark, Jeffrey W. "How America Saves Report 2023." Vanguard, 2023. https://institutional.vanguard.com/content/dam/inst/iig-transformation/has/2023/pdf/has-insights/how-america-saves-report-2023.pdf.

Chapter 4

1. Gillespie, Lane. "Bankrate's Annual Emergency Fund Report." Bankrate, June 22, 2023. https://www.bankrate.com/banking/savings/emergency-savings-report/.
2. Depietro, Andrew and Gaby Lapera. "Average American Debt by Age and Generation: 2022: Credit Karma." Intuit Credit Karma, June 22, 2023. https://www.creditkarma.com/insights/i/average-debt-by-age.
3. Jones, Jenn. "Average Car Payment and Auto Loan Statistics 2023." LendingTree, June 27, 2023. https://www.lendingtree.com/auto/debt-statistics.
4. "Global Intelligence Automotive Adspend Forecasts." Zenith, 2019. https://www.zenithmedia.com/wp-content/uploads/2019/03/Automotive-adspend-forecasts-2019-executive-summary.pdf.
5. DiFurio, Dom. "Here's How U.S. Credit Card Debt Has Changed in Five Years." Experian, February 15, 2023. https://www.experian.com/blogs/ask-experian/how-credit-card-debt-has-changed-over-last-5-years/.
6. Dilworth, Kelly. "Average Credit Card Interest Rates: Week of Dec. 21, 2022." CreditCards.com, August 3, 2023. https://www.creditcards.com/news/rate-report/.
7. Roney, Luke. "Here's a Guy Who Has 1,497 Credit Cards." USA Today, January 10, 2016. https://www.usatoday.com/story/money/2016/01/10/credit-cards-newser/78592058.
8. Leonhardt, Megan. "55% of Americans with Credit Cards Have Debt—Here's How Much It Could Cost You." CNBC, June 5, 2019. https://www.cnbc.com/2019/05/17/55-percent-of-americans-have-credit-card-debt.html.
9. Helhoski, Anna and Eliza Haverstock. "How Many Americans Have Student Loan Debt?" NerdWallet, January 19, 2023. https://www.nerdwallet.com/article/loans/student-loans/how-many-americans-have-student-loan-debt; "Tuition Inflation." Finaid, July 7, 2022. https://finaid.org/savings/tuition-inflation/; Marcus, Jon. "Panicked Universities in Search of Students Are Adding Thousands of New Majors." The Hechinger Report, April 8, 2021. https://

hechingerreport.org/panicked-universities-in-search-of-students-are-adding-thousands-of-new-majors/; Abel, Jaison R. and Richard Deitz. "Agglomeration and Job Matching Among College Graduates." Federal Reserve Bank of New York, December 2012. https://www.newyorkfed.org/medialibrary/media/research/staff_reports/sr587.pdf.

10. McMahon, Tim. "Long Term U.S. Inflation." InflationData.com, April 1, 2014. https://inflationdata.com/Inflation/Inflation_Rate/Long_Term_Inflation.asp.
11. White, Martha C. "The Worst College Majors for Student Loans." Time, December 4, 2014. https://time.com/3616463/student-loans-college-majors/.
12. Hershbein, Brad, Ben Harris, and Melissa S. Kearney. "Major Decisions: Graduates' Earnings Growth and Debt Repayment." The Hamilton Project, March 27, 2023. https://www.hamiltonproject.org/publication/paper/major-decisions-graduates-earnings-growth-and-debt-repayment/.
13. Whitler, Kimberly A. "A New Study on Fortune 100 CEOS: The (Surprising) Undergraduate Institutions They Attended." Forbes, October 12, 2019. https://www.forbes.com/sites/kimberlywhitler/2019/09/07/a-new-study-on-fortune-100-ceos-what-undergraduate-institutions-did-they-attend/?sh=3451b69b3308.
14. Valbrun, Marjorie. "Nacubo Report Shows Tuition-Discounting Trend Continuing Unabated." Inside Higher Ed | Higher Education News, Events and Jobs, May 9, 2019. https://www.insidehighered.com/news/2019/05/10/nacubo-report-shows-tuition-discounting-trend-continuing-unabated.

Chapter 5

1. Wells, Libby. "Brick-and-Mortar Banks vs. Online Banks: Pros and Cons." Bankrate, January 24, 2023. https://www.bankrate.com/banking/savings/online-vs-brick-and-mortar-banks/.
2. Wells, "Brick-and-Mortar Banks vs. Online Banks."

3. Goldberg, Matthew. "Best Savings Accounts for October 2023." Bankrate, October 12, 2023. https://www.bankrate.com/banking/savings/rates/.

Chapter 6

1. "Sort by Popularity—Most Popular Movies and TV Shows Tagged with Keyword 'Saving-the-World.'" IMDb, October 12, 2023. https://www.imdb.com/search/keyword/?keywords=saving-the-world.
2. "TAXPAYER RELIEF ACT OF 1997." GovInfo | U.S. Government Publishing Office, August 5, 1997. https://www.govinfo.gov/content/pkg/PLAW-105publ34/pdf/PLAW-105publ34.pdf.
3. Fidelity Viewpoints. "How to Plan for Rising Health Care Costs." Fidelity, June 21, 2023. https://www.fidelity.com/viewpoints/personal-finance/plan-for-rising-health-care-costs.
4. Fronstin, Paul. "Health Savings Account Balances, Contributions, Distributions, and Other Vital Statistics, 2017: Statistics from the EBRI HSA Database." EBRI, October 15, 2018. https://www.ebri.org/content/health-savings-account-balances-contributions-distributions-and-other-vital-statistics-2017-statistics-from-the-ebri-hsa-database.

Chapter 7

1. Adamczyk, Alicia. "This Is When People Start Saving for Retirement—and When They Actually Should." CNBC, September 4, 2019. https://www.cnbc.com/2019/09/04/the-age-when-americans-start-saving-for-retirement.html.

Chapter 8

1. "10 Spooky Facts about Retirement." LIMRA.com, October 31, 2019. https://www.limra.com/en/newsroom/industry-trends/2019/10-spooky-facts-about-retirement/.

2. Ramsey, Dave. *Baby Steps Millionaires: How Ordinary People Built Extraordinary Wealth—and How You Can Too.* Franklin, Tenn.: Ramsey Press, The Lampo Group, LLC, 2022.

Chapter 9

1. Hess, Abigail J. "Here's Why Lottery Winners Go Broke." CNBC, August 25, 2017. https://www.cnbc.com/2017/08/25/heres-why-lottery-winners-go-broke.html.

Chapter 10

1. O'Neill, Aaron. "United States: Life Expectancy 1860–2020." Statista, June 21, 2022. https://www.statista.com/statistics/1040079/life-expectancy-united-states-all-time/.
2. "The Top 10 Benefits of 529 Plans." Savingforcollege.com, May 11, 2023. https://www.savingforcollege.com/intro-to-529s/name-the-top-7-benefits-of-529-plans.
3. Buffett, Warren E. "Berkshire Hathaway Inc. Letter to Shareholders." Berkshire Hathaway Inc., February 28, 2005. https://www.berkshirehathaway.com/letters/2004ltr.pdf.

Chapter 11

1. Stone, Arthur A., Joseph E. Schwartz, Joan E. Broderick, and Angus Deaton. "A Snapshot of the Age Distribution of Psychological Well-Being in the United States." PNAS, May 17, 2010. https://www.pnas.org/doi/10.1073/pnas.1003744107.

Chapter 12

1. Gillespie, Lane. "Bankrate's Annual Emergency Fund Report." Bankrate, June 22, 2023. https://www.bankrate.com/banking/savings/emergency-savings-report/.
2. Gillespie, "Bankrate's Annual Emergency Fund Report."

3. Elkins, Kathleen. "Here's How Many Working Americans Aren't Saving Any Money for Retirement or Emergencies at All." CNBC, March 14, 2019. https://www.cnbc.com/2019/03/14/heres-how-many-americans-are-not-saving-any-money-for-emergencies-or-retirement-at-all.html.

Chapter 13

1. Das, Anupreeta. "Buffett's Crisis-Lending Haul Reaches $10 Billion." The Wall Street Journal, October 7, 2013. https://www.wsj.com/articles/SB10001424052702304441404579119742104942198.
2. Chiglinsky, Katherine. "Berkshire Cash Pile Hits a Record $122 Billion." Bloomberg.com, August 3, 2019. https://www.bloomberg.com/news/articles/2019-08-03/buffett-s-cash-pile-hits-record-as-berkshire-holds-122-billion#xj4y7vzkg.
3. Fronstin, Paul. "Health Savings Account Balances, Contributions, Distributions, and Other Vital Statistics, 2017: Statistics from the EBRI HSA Database." EBRI, October 15, 2018. https://www.ebri.org/content/health-savings-account-balances-contributions-distributions-and-other-vital-statistics-2017-statistics-from-the-ebri-hsa-database.

Index

L

M

About the Author

Photo by Tausha Dickinson

Brian Preston, CPA, CFP®, PFS, is the founder and host of *The Money Guy Show* and Managing Partner and co-founder of Abound Wealth Management. He started podcasting as a passion project in 2006 out of pure excitement to share and educate the masses on building abundance through sound financial decisions. Fast-forward to today, and *The Money Guy Show* is its own enterprise, helping millions of individuals build wealth and own their time. When he's not busy making the wonderful world of finance accessible to the public, you can find him spending time with his wife and two daughters, watching the latest movies, traveling with family and friends, and cheering for the University of Georgia Bulldogs.